Paranormal Fright

Diana Formisano Willett

authorHOUSE®

AuthorHouse™
1663 Liberty Drive
Bloomington, IN 47403
www.authorhouse.com
Phone: 1-800-839-8640

Published by AuthorHouse   03/22/2013

ISBN: 978-1-4817-3269-7 (sc)
ISBN: 978-1-4817-3268-0 (hc)
ISBN: 978-1-4817-3267-3 (e)

Library of Congress Control Number: 2013905222

CONTENTS

CHAPTER 1

THE VORTEX

Why does the soul return after death? No one really knows.

Are the souls protecting their loved ones here on Earth? There is no real answer to this question.

We all lived before we were here. This Earth is our mortal existence. The soul returns to Earth in certain circumstances. I have verifiable photos of spirits returning to Earth from the spirit world.

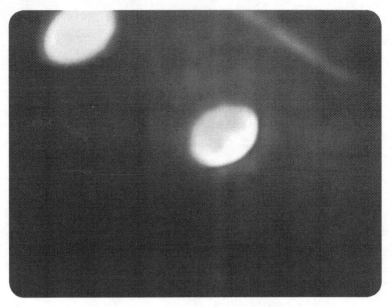

TWO ORBS IN THE LIVING ROOM

Now, let's discuss what a vortex is, how it plays an important part in learning about the spirit world, and how a spirit can come back to Earth. A vortex is the vehicle by which a spirit enters this world. A large volume of energy is required for a ghost to make itself seen or heard. A vortex is what can be seen through photographs and video footage; the vortex results from an energy surge great enough for a spirit to manifest. Most of these vortices are circular or whirling in motion. They are seen in paranormally active locations, such as my home. These vortices are momentary doorways or portals to another realm that allows entities or other paranormal phenomena to come into this world. Some researchers of the paranormal think these vortices are linked to the Earth's own electromagnetic field, which, at least in part, determines when these portals or doorways open and close. I have captured a vortex on video. The vortex was a funnel-shaped whirling mass of energy and light that happened suddenly in

November 2009 and disappeared just as fast. These vortices are also called warps. People are afraid to walk near or into them. You could become lost forever!

When a vortex appears or when the spirit or spirits enter this dimension, you can hear some type of explosion. It sounds like a giant boom, as though a bomb went off in the distance. I think this is how the spirits enter this dimension from the other realm. My son and I experienced this sound one night in November. I had ordered a pizza, and while eating it in the dining room we heard a boom outside the house. At first, I thought someone's car or other device had malfunctioned. I then heard some type of noise in the living room. I paid no attention to it and proceeded to eat the pizza and clean up the table. I then got ready to go to bed. In the morning, I always view video camera footage from the previous night to see if there was any paranormal activity. I noticed a strange mist coming from the top of the living room near the ceiling. This mist was moving and spinning back and forth in the living room. I could not believe what I saw. I could see my husband's face in this mist. I could see him yelling and talking to someone. I could see another entity in the mist also. The face looked like a skeleton. This was a vortex. This is their portal into this dimension. I also saw an orb enter the vortex. The mist was there the entire night. I could still see it in the living room the next morning. Finally, in midmorning, it left the house. Wow—what a tremendous sight to see! I have the video footage of this vortex on a DVD. Members of the North Shore Paranormal Society think it is, in fact, a vortex. Now we have proof that spirits exist and come back into this dimension through a portal called a vortex.

FACE IN THE VORTEX

Why does my husband still return? He is not at rest. Why, I still don't know. Did something happen the day he died that continues to upset him even in death? Did something contribute to his death? I tried to get him back into the hospital that morning before I went to work. He did not want to go back to the emergency room to be checked. His thumb and the rest of his hand were red and extremely swollen. I remember that Monday morning he was trying to write some checks and had difficulty writing because of the pain. I told him I would write the checks out, but he was extremely stubborn and proceeded to write the checks himself even though his writing was very shaky. I was still trying to persuade him to go to the hospital that morning before I left for work. I told him to call 911 and said I would ride with him in the ambulance since I work at the hospital and could just go right to work after he entered the emergency room. Well, I could not convince him, so I proceeded to leave for work. The visiting nurse was coming over at 11:00 a.m., so I told him I would call him then. I got busy at work and called him at noon. The nurse had just left, and my husband told me the nurse thought he could see his doctor on an outpatient visit to clear up the gout that continued to return in his hand and thumb. I did not agree with this and told him that as soon as I got home that night, we were going back to the hospital. I think his death was so unexpected and so quick that he does not want to cross over. He continues to haunt my house constantly. It has now been seven and a half years since his death. My husband, Brad, died February 7, 2005, and there are still hauntings here. Of course, we know that others come with him via the portal. I wonder what other entities could also be coming here. I wonder if there are ghosts from other planets who can also come here to Earth. This is a question that is almost impossible to answer. I hope to eventually get to the bottom of this and see if it is possible.

Let's start at the beginning of this story. Let's go back to my childhood and see why these occurrences are happening to me. Why do the dead continue to come here? Do I have a connection with the afterlife? I was saved from drowning when I was a little girl in New York City. I know there was some heavenly intervention. A hand came down and pulled me up from the water to the top of the pool, where I was safe. God or some angel was watching out for me. My mother told me it was my guardian angel. My experiences with the beyond continue to this day.

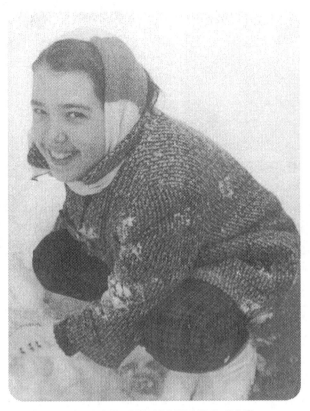

AUTHOR AT 10 YEARS OLD

I would like to elaborate on these vortices, which are the vehicle into this world from the spirit world. Many people have photographs of these vortices. They are real. They can be dangerous, because you can get lost in them as with the Bermuda Triangle. Planes, ships, and people have vanished from the location called the Bermuda Triangle. Numerous books and articles have been written about this extraordinary place. Could it be the site of some type of paranormal activity, or could it be some type of alien home under the water? No one knows, and no one can answer this question. I read it could be strong tides in this area that have covered up these ships or made planes go down. This is still being investigated.

Please do not think this is a joke. This area is a very dangerous place, and you must be extremely cautious crossing over it.

I have found some help with this vortex situation. On my Twitter page the North Shore Paranormal Society agreed to look at my DVD of a vortex and let me know what they thought. My friend at the North Shore Paranormal Society is Danny, and he e-mailed me the results of their investigation of the DVD. Here are the results:

The society believes it is a vortex based on the fact that it appears to be solid in the middle. This vortex is surrounded by concentric rings of light, and the light is pulsing on the video, which suggests rotation. These are all clear indicators of a vortex. There are tests that can verify a vortex, but they are measurements of the wavelength and type of waves that were present in the video. Since we cannot predict when or where these things will appear, it is almost impossible to set up these tests. The easiest and most definitive test also cannot be performed, which would be to shine a laser light through the vortex. If the light appears on the wall behind it, then you have a manifestation and *not* a vortex. If the light disappears into the center, then you have a definite portal.

Dan from the Paranormal Society told me that I definitely have some sort of opening based on what I have witnessed and experienced. These vortices are the centers of the paranormal disturbances I have been experiencing for the past seven years. What to do now is a mystery for sure.

How do you capture a vortex spinning and then test this anomaly? It is almost impossible to see it with the naked eye. This particular vortex was present in the living room all day and all night, and we did not detect anything until I happened to look at the video footage the next day after I returned home. The only sign of something entering this atmosphere is the sound it makes when it enters. It sounded like an explosion and a tremendous bang. These situations seem to manifest more in the cold months than in the summertime. I don't know the significance of this, but I am investigating why it seems to happen in the wintertime.

I must tell you of an experience my son had in his bedroom one day while I was at work. He was taking a nap downstairs in his bedroom and felt himself spinning around. He was in the vortex and felt himself spinning around in the room. He was able to get out of the vortex and saw a girl, who stood in his room for a moment and then disappeared. He told me after getting out of this vortex that he had a terrible headache. This is quite concerning since he could have been taken up and never come back.

I would like to discuss the nature of vile vortices. *Vile vortices* refers to twelve geographic areas that are alleged by Ivan Sanderson to have been the sites of mysterious disappearances. He identified them in a 1972 article titled "The Twelve Devil's Graveyards Around the World," which was published by *Saga* magazine. Sanderson asserts that twelve vortices are situated along particular lines of latitude. The best known of the vortices is the Bermuda Triangle. Some of the others are the Algerian Megaliths to the south of Timbuktu; the Indus Valley in Pakistan, especially the city of Mohenjo Daro; Hamakulia Volcano in Hawaii; the Devil's Sea near Japan; and the South Atlantic Anomaly. Five of the vortices are on the same latitude to the south of the equator; five are on the same latitude to the north. You and Ivan Sanderson must make your own decisions about his and other people's theories of these places around the world. I believe there is a link with the paranormal, a suspension of the laws of physics, or activity by extraterrestrial beings. Many people and cultures around the world also suspect these reasons. The other two places are the North and South poles. The vortices are linked to some type of subtle matter energy, ley lines, or electromagnetic aberration. I strongly agree with the latter explanation. Three of these alleged vortices are the Bermuda Triangle, the Devil's Sea, and Easter Island. Of course, this is a hypothesis for many disappearances. Others believe that these incidences have been either inaccurately reported or embellished by authors, and numerous official agencies have gone on record as saying that the number and nature of these disappearances to be similar to any other area of ocean, many remained unexplained despite considerable investigation. The Gulf Stream flows through the triangle, and after leaving the Gulf of Mexico, its current of five to six knots may have played a part in a number of disappearances. According to the Coast Guard Reports 120 boats and ships disappear in a year without a trace.

One mysterious disappearance was that of Flight 19, reported in 1945. A group of five U.S. Navy TBM Avenger bombers on a training mission went missing. An article titled "The Lost Patrol," by Allen W. Eckert, claimed that the flight leader had been heard saying, "We are entering white water. Nothing seems right. We don't know where we are. The water is green, not white." It was also claimed that officials at the navy board of inquiry said that the planes "flew off to Mars." "The Lost Patrol" was the first to connect the supernatural to Flight 19, but it would take another author, Vincent Gaddis, writing in the February 1964 issue of *Argosy* magazine, to take Flight

19 together with other mysterious disappearances and place it under the umbrella of a new catchy name, "The Deadly Bermuda Triangle." He built on that article with a more detailed book titled *Invisible Horizons* the next year.

There were other authors: John Wallace Spencer (*Limbo of the Lost* 1969), Charles Berlitz (*The Bermuda Triangle* 1974), Richard Winer (*The Devil's Triangle* 1974), and many others, all keeping to some of the same supernatural elements outlined by Eckert.

Many people also reported some type of fog called an electrical fog. Others have reported seeing portals opening in cloudy skies, strange swirling lights sometimes accompanied by sounds, temporal distortions, electromagnetic distortions called electrical fog that can cause a time storm, and the disappearances of planes and ships. There is something about this fog that is important and gives one the sense of the paranormal. I think something unexplained is definitely happening in this region of the Atlantic, and I feel this is the same unexplained phenomenon as the portal in my house. I feel this can all be tied in to the same type of electromagnetic phenomenon that happens only when conditions are right for these portals to arise. These unexplained forces were even used for an idea by Steven Spielberg in the movie *Close Encounters of the Third Kind,* which features the lost Flight 19 as an alien abduction.

Now let's talk about the Devil's Sea, which has the same paranormal effects as the Bermuda Triangle. It is in a region of the Pacific around Miyake Island, about 100 kilometers south of Tokyo. The name Devil's Island used by Japanese fishermen does not appear on nautical maps. There is a lot of volcanic activity around the area, and the underwater volcano could obliterate a ship without a trace.

The Sargasso Sea is in the east side of the triangle in the middle of the Atlantic. It houses a few small islands and masses of clumped, floating seaweed. A warm water current within it swirls clockwise, affecting the weather of the area, keeping it calm and steamy. Having little wind, this area greatly affects unpowered ships. Christopher Columbus and his crew sighted unexplained dancing lights on the horizon in this area. They wandered around for more than a week before finally sighting land.

Another strange place is called the Michigan Triangle. This triangle is over central Lake Michigan. One side stretches from the town of Ludington to Benton Harbor in Michigan; another links from Benton Harbor to Manitowoc, Wisconsin; the final side connects Manitowoc back to Ludington.

There are numerous stories of strange creatures; unexplained vanishings; time standing still, slowing to a crawl, or speeding up; and other weird happenings. In a well-documented case, Captain George R. Donnor, who commanded the Great Lakes freighter *O. M. McFarland,* disappeared on the ship. On the night of April 28, 1937, the captain took to his cabin, with instructions to be awakened as the ship drew near the port. About three hours later, with Port Washington growing close, the second mate appeared at the captain's cabin, prepared to awake him, but found no one. He and the crew searched the ship, but the captain was never seen again. The mate reported that the cabin door was locked from the inside, adding to the mystery of the triangle. The ship was in the dead center of the triangle when the captain disappeared.

Portals or windows to another reality most likely exist. There are specific locations for them. As you know, the Bermuda Triangle is one of these locations. The Bermuda Triangle is associated with missing ships and planes, and there are even sightings of UFOs. The area described as the Bermuda Triangle is very large, but the actual portal that opens up may be small (perhaps the size of a football field, as suggested in many books). These portals or openings to another reality may be like wormholes, and people and objects may be caught between these dimensions where time is at a standstill. I believe these portals act as some type of barrier to protect the two realities from contaminating each other. This dimensional portal of the Bermuda Triangle is probably used by the intelligence behind UFOs to enter this world. UFO intelligence may wait until these portals naturally open for them to enter this world. They leave this Earth when the portal opens again. This theory would explain why these UFOs stay in a certain location on Earth and then reappear months or years later in a regular cycle. They may be able to trigger these portal openings by generating an electromagnetic pulse, forcing a natural portal to open. I have witnessed the sound of this portal opening from the spirit world to our world by a large noise—a tremendous blast. It sounds as though a window opens to this world by the sound of an explosion. It could be that this electromagnetic pulse opens with a boom as I hear when the portal opens up to this world. Research into the Bermuda Triangle has shown that these portals open in the months of March, July, August, and October. The number of paranormal cases seem to peak in these particular months. Here in my home, November is also a very active month for paranormal activity. I have captured that portal in my house in the month of November, when it gets colder in this region. The cold seems to increase the paranormal activity here. I, of course, do not know the physics behind this, but I am sure it will be investigated to determine if the electromagnetic pulse gets stronger or portals are easier to open in the winter months.

Just as the Bermuda Triangle is marked as a dangerous place for paranormal and UFO portals, the Devil's Sea, off the east coast of Japan, is another such area. In 1970, the Japanese government sent a research vessel with scientists and crew out to investigate the Devil's Sea. This particular research ship along with the crew must have found something, because they disappeared without a trace. There was an extensive air-sea search, and not even a small piece of debris was found. The Devil's Sea and the Bermuda Triangle area emit very strong electromagnetic pulses and cause compasses to spin out of control. Swirling clouds, intense electrical storms, and waterspouts that appear without any type of warning have all been reported. This rotating and swirling air and water is most likely caused by a vortex when a dimensional window opens or closes. These vortices are the doorways to the spirit world. I believe there is a miniature one in my home based on the paranormal activity in this home and orbs captured on my video camera.

Chapter 2

Another Dimension

There are scientists here on Earth who believe there are ten higher dimensions. They think we live in the third dimension. According to this theory, the universe is held together by strings that vibrate at different frequencies. It is possible that these higher dimensions exist, but because they vibrate at frequencies that we cannot perceive, we do not typically know or think they exist during our day-to-day lives. The strange events that occur all over the world (such as in the Bermuda Triangle) and the reports of ghost hauntings, combined with intense scientific curiosity, means that entirely new planes of being may yet be discovered.

It has been theorized that even aliens—and perhaps ghosts or shadow people as well—are actually beings from another dimension of time and space beyond our own. I have seen these shadow people right in my own home, standing on the stairway. They look like human beings, but their features look strange. The nose resembles that of a human being, but they are not quite human looking. One particular shadow person looked like my husband, but the nose was distorted. The nose was very narrow and artificial looking, as was the face. It smiled and then disappeared. The shadow it cast was extremely dark and black, four to five feet in front of this being. The black it cast was a black I have never seen before. I also have seen two distinct black shadows coming from the house on a November afternoon at approximately 2:30 p.m. They were in the driveway, and my video camera picked up the images. First, you could see a shadow being walking in the driveway and then turning and walking to the back of the house. Then another shadow being walked in the driveway and walked to the back of the house where the first shadow being went. Very scary, this was. Why do these strange creatures visit us? They may appear as shadows, apparitions, or creatures from another planet piloting strange, unidentified aircraft in the skies. Are these creatures trying to study us or are they just taking a tour of Earth? You decide!

This other dimension I want to talk about is where the spirits go when they pass over. I have seen a spirit walk through my living room wall while I was in the kitchen. This wall acts as a doorway from their dimension into ours. When we die, we go to another realm unless we have received the gift of the heavenly realm. The borders between these realms are very vague. Who can say where one ends and the other realm begins?

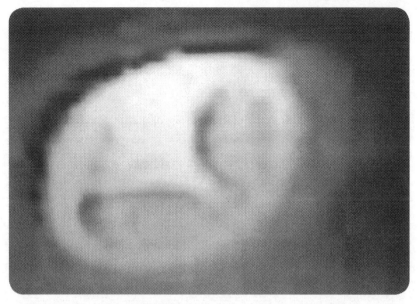

MY HUSBAND'S FACE IN ORB

There is definitely "another dimension." Parallel dimensions are believed to be other forms of existence. Spirits and other entities can travel to our world. There is something called the 3:00 a.m. theory. Are the veils the thinnest at 3:00 a.m.? Jesus died at 3:00 p.m., so 3:00 a.m. would be the polar opposite. This is just a theory of paranormal investigators, that between 11:00 p.m. and 4:00 a.m., the veils are the thinnest, allowing easy travel not just at one particular time (3:00 a.m.). I am continually haunted, and these times are correct. I am especially aware of the hauntings between 11:00 p.m. and 1:00 a.m. I have had some scary times around midnight. Just last week, I woke up and looked at the clock. It was 12:15 a.m. From my bedroom I heard pots rattling downstairs in my kitchen. I had happened to put some pots on the floor next to my cabinets. I heard someone or something bang into the pots and then put one down on the floor. I immediately went downstairs. I was scared to death to see what was going on down there. No one was there—or at least I could not see anyone. I did see two of the pots turned over and one small pot placed near the cabinet where my phone was. I went back to bed and, of course, could not sleep the entire night. Two days later another strange, terrifying incident happened. I was watching television in my bedroom when I heard a tremendous crash in my office, which is near the bedroom. I got up and saw two crates that I had filled with electrical wires thrown to the floor. My son and I immediately cleaned up the mess and wondered who could be doing this. This happened on October 5, and I remembered that my mother-in-law had died on October 3, 1989. Is someone trying to tell us something? This also happened one year after my mother died. I was upstairs in my bedroom when I heard the blender in the kitchen go on. My son was in his playpen and started to scream at the noise. I ran downstairs and pulled the plug of the blender out of the socket. It had not been plugged in when I went upstairs. I happened to be standing near the telephone where the calendar was. I happened to look at the calendar, and the date was May 6. May 6 was the date of my mother's death. She wanted me to remember that she died on that date. Spirits want to help us and try to tell us things that we really need to know. Listen to them and see what they are saying to you. Try not to be afraid, although I admit that at times, I get quite fearful.

This other dimension, as we know, is composed of ghosts and spirits. What is a ghost? Ghosts are apparitions of dead people. I have seen my husband appear in my bedroom window since his death. I was coming home about 6:00 p.m. and got out of the car in my driveway. I happened to look up at my bedroom window and saw his image standing in the window. He looked young—about thirty years old. He was all in black. He stared at me for a second and disappeared. I was terrified. So I do know that apparitions are real. Ghosts appear in their human form and in places they visited or lived before their death. Ghosts can appear in three different forms: ectoplasm, ecto-mist, and a full-bodied apparition. An ecto-mist or paranormal mist is a swirling energy that resembles fog illuminated by light. It has been captured in still photos and video and is usually white and luminous in nature, although occasionally it is red. It is also called ectoplasm. I have just viewed a new orb entering the living room and a red colored ecto-mist seen on the camera. It was by the sofa. This was seen after the orb disappeared from the picture. I have been experiencing more hauntings now in November than in other months. Why, I am not quite sure yet. Typically, this ecto-mist is more easily viewed through video, as I have documented on my DVD. Cameras capture this paranormal mist more often than video recorders. The third form is an apparition: a ghostly figure or the act of appearing or becoming visible unexpectedly. Often at times, a spirit of the deceased will take on the physical form from their past life. I got out of the car and looked up at my bedroom window to see my husband standing in the window looking at me. I was terrified to go into that house alone. I proceeded to enter the house and go up to the bedroom, but no one was there. This apparition appeared in the first few months of my husband's death. My husband looked young—his eyes moved to look at me, but the body did not move at all. He did not smile or make any type of expression, and then disappeared. It was a very scary situation in this house, and it continues to this day.

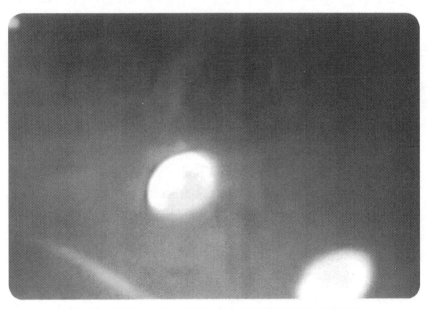

ORBS WITH MIST SURROUNDING THEM

CHAPTER 3

SPIRITS

In reality, there is no death. The body dies, but the soul or spirit lives on. The soul is the incorporeal essence of a person, living thing, or even an object. We are made up of energy, and this energy is your soul. The soul is very powerful. One night, I found myself in the living room in the air, swaying back and forth. This was my astral body. An aura is associated with the astral body.

I could see how powerful the soul is, as my energy was causing the drapes to move with force. The drapes were blowing from the energy that was my soul. Just remember, the soul lives forever but not in its human form. Your astral body moves from corner to corner in a room. It does not fly as much in the middle of a room but moves from corner to corner. As an apparition appears, you can hear movement in the corners of a room. I can verify this by my own experience in my bedroom. I was sleeping one night and heard noise from the corner near the window to my bedroom. I paid no attention, as I did not see anything, and proceeded to go back to sleep. I woke up in the middle of the night and saw an apparition standing next to my bed where my husband used to sleep. It was an apparition of a young man who looked about thirty years old. He was smiling at me and wanted to hand me some type of envelope. As I woke up, I saw this man and started to scream, but I could not move. I was absolutely terrified. It looked like he was laughing, and then he disappeared. There was also movement in the other corner of my bedroom near the wall next to my dresser. I heard a woman imitate me one evening. Apparitions listen and imitate others! My son hears these spirits when he takes a nap during the day while I am at work. He told me he heard a voice calling him but that it sounded like my voice. Spirits can imitate the living. Spirits have powers you don't know about. A paranormal expert I was talking to told me spirits cannot go over running waters (like the ocean), but this is not true. When my husband first died, I took a cruise in May 2005 and he appeared along with some other spirit in my cabin. So, spirits can move over running waters. I can verify this! A hand came over to me as I was sleeping in the cabin and took my covers to cover me up. Then, this hand waved good-bye to me and left. The spirits can definitely appear over water if they want to, but why do they return? Is it because of me that they keep appearing or trying to communicate with me? It seems that this is the case, as they continue to appear when there is some type of upset in my life. When everything is going fine, they seem to be quiet and do not come back.

SPIRIT FACE IN WINDOW

The spirit is powerful and highly intelligent. This intelligence greatly surpasses human intelligence. Ghosts or spirits return to haunt homes where they were either residents or were familiar with the property. Sometimes, supernatural activity inside homes is associated with violent or tragic events. This can include a murder, an accidental death, a suicide, or maybe a wrongful death. I believe my husband's death was a wrongful death based on the circumstances in the house. Something happened that day when I was at work. I will not elaborate on this at this time but will get back to it later.

Many cultures and religions believe the essence of a being, such as the soul, continues to exist after death. Some philosophical or religious views argue that the spirits of those who have died have not "passed over" and are trapped inside the property where their memories and energy are strong. As soon as my husband died, we started to have paranormal activity in the house. We do not have poltergeists, which are nasty ghosts that manifest themselves by moving or influencing objects. That is one thing that I do not have to deal with, which is good. There are, of course, other entities that are spirits but they have other names you may not be familiar with. One is called the jinn. The jinn are ethereal beings. They are said to be made from smokeless fire, which is plasma: the fourth state of being. According to legend, the jinn were placed between the universe's light and matter by the angels. Ancient Islamic stories denote the jinn as spirits that in their normal form look half human and half reptile. They can be channeled through a human host and often identify themselves as extraterrestrials, angels, or loved ones who have died to get the confidence of the people in a channeling session. We share this planet with a multitude of unseen beings. Just because the majority of humans do not believe in these entities certainly does not prove that they do *not* exist. They certainly do! I have seen for myself shadow people, orbs, a strange entity appearing at my bedside in the air, apparitions in my room, the soul light in my room, and a vast number of strange and scary occurrences. Before the death of my husband, there was no way on Earth I would have believed in these things. Now I know they exist.

Let's get back to talking about the jinn. This type of spirit was created by God from smokeless fire, as I said above. They are separate from humans and the angels. The word *jinn* is from the Arabic and means "the hidden." This is what they appear to want to do: stay hidden and cover up their true identity. The jinn can be agents of good or evil, but most are evil and enjoy punishing humans because they feel God has placed humankind in a better dimension. The ancients believed that any type of accidents, disease, or untimely deaths were the result of the wrathful jinn. The jinn are said to possess the power to heal, change shape, control the elements of nature, create illusions, and also control the mind of those who accept them. *Beware the jinn!*

The soul/spirit will continue on after physical death. The spirit world will wait until another soul enters heaven and will greet you when you enter the kingdom of heaven. This is called your "appointed time." I was in contact with many psychics when my husband passed away. I was very upset that I was not at home when he died. He came back from the hospital one week before he died. He returned home on Wednesday and died the following Monday. I wanted him to return to the hospital that Monday, but he refused and wanted to wait for the visiting nurse, Jennifer, to come over. I tried again and again to persuade him to go to the hospital before I left for work. I told him I would call 911 and go with him to the hospital, because I worked there. He said no, and I proceeded to go to work. I called him around noon and he told me the nurse had just left. She did not think he needed to go to the hospital, because his thumb was not that swollen and she thought his physician could care for him on an outpatient basis. He had developed some type of gout/cellulitis of the extremity. It flared up again during the weekend, and by Monday was so swollen he could barely write. Well, he did not listen to me, and I called him again around 3:20 p.m. and he answered the phone. I asked him, "How are you doing?" and he replied, "No good." I asked him what was wrong. He told me he could not move from the chair and go downstairs to the bathroom. He was waiting for oxygen to be delivered at 4:00 p.m. I told him to cancel the delivery since he was not feeling well, and to wait until I came home. He told me he could cancel it and I told him, "As soon as I come home, you are to go back to the hospital." I called again around 5:15 p.m., and a police officer answered. I asked to speak to my husband and asked why they were there. He told me the paramedics were working on my husband and to come home immediately. Well, when I came home, I found him dead on the floor, covered with a sheet. The police waited there until I came home, and I had to call an undertaker to pick up the body. I always felt I should have been there, but a particular psychic told me "this was his appointed time" and that was that. Nothing in the world could have changed it. You were *not* supposed to be there when he died, the psychic said. So when people feel very bad and are longing for their loved ones who have died, just remember it was their appointed time. Only God controls this, and no one else can change it. It must be accepted, and you are not to look back and feel bad about the fact that you were not there at the time of death. I remember looking at my husband's face when I took the sheet and pulled it back. I saw that his eyes were shut, but they looked glued shut—very tightly shut, as though they were going into the skin. He still had the tube in his mouth that the paramedics had used to administer oxygen when they intubated him. One hand was in a fist, and he had a bandage on the right arm where the paramedics had administered a medication. I saw a red line from the bandaged site to the hand. I don't know if this came from the infected thumb area or the medication caused it. It was a red line that extended up the arm. I don't know the significance of it. It looked to me like some type of cellulitis extending to the rest of the body, but I was not sure. I tried not to think about it anymore and to continue my life, but the memory of it is still very vivid. It was a horrible site for me to see. Thank God my son was not there when he died. He had an apartment and did not know of my husband's death until I took him home that night and told him his father had died. It was a terrible night.

WEDDING DAY

Let's get back to what spirits, ghosts, and the soul really are. We know that these spirits and ghost come from another dimension. Throughout history there has been evidence that this other dimension exists. The spinning vortex in my living room documents the evidence of another dimension and how the spirits enter this dimension. We are living in the third dimension, according to scientists here on Earth. Spirits, shadow people, and other entities are beings from another dimension of time and space who, for their own mysterious reasons, plan to come to our dimension from time to time. They may appear as fleeting shadows, vaporous apparitions, or some type of creatures piloting strange aircraft as documented by UFO reports throughout the world. Aliens from another dimension may also haunt our Earth and appear as ghosts, according to many paranormal reports. One day, I decided to turn on my digital recorder in my bedroom and go to the mall. I wanted to see if there was anything coming into the house or already in the house when I was not home. I left the digital recorder on my dresser and left for the mall. I was there for about three hours and then returned home. I then turned the recorder off and later that evening decided to put it on to see if there was any activity in the house when I left. At first, you hear just the sound of the recorder, but then all of a sudden you can hear some type of static going on and off on the recorder. It is as though something is coming into the bedroom and then leaving again. I kept listening to the recorder and then I heard some type of bang in the bedroom, as though someone or something had hit the wall. It is always one bang, not more than that. I heard my jewelry being touched but no other sounds until I heard a rather strange voice coming from the recorder. It sounded like a robot voice and it said, "You will have millions." I could not believe my ears and tried to get the voice back on the recorder. I kept reversing but was not able to hear it again. I went forward on the recorder and then again in reverse, but I could not hear that voice again. I finally rewound the entire tape and listened again from the beginning. I heard it again, but this time it was faint, not as loud as it had been before. I don't understand this, but when I touched the tape and reversed it, I could not hear the voice clearly again. It now sounded as though it was coming from downstairs—in the distance. Since I could not hear the voice again after reversing the tape, I just forgot about it, but it sounded like an alien voice, and in my office room, we saw fingerprints that looked alien, not human. I really wished I had had a camera in my bedroom like the other three cameras I have installed. I am sure I would have caught some type of figure.

As far as spirits are concerned, there are essentially two kinds: those who are inhabiting a body and those who are not. Of those who are inhabiting bodies, there are many different kinds of spirits. Those spirits that inhabit the human body can also inhabit an animal's body. In regard to the human spirits who are not currently in a body, some have not made the journey to the other dimension (called the afterlife). These are called lost souls, and they need help finding the light. They may be afraid of some type of punishment and so do not want to be judged.

There are also spirits who are not in bodies—or who are not in human bodies, at any rate. There is also an entire realm of spirits, such as sprites, fairies, and mythical beasts and creatures that exist and are very near our dimension. The inhabitants of this realm can see us, but most humans cannot see them. I say "most humans" because I did have an experience with one of these spirits in my bedroom about four years ago. I believe the spirit I saw in my room is called a deva, which is a nonphysical being. A deva is a nature spirit, a fluidic, open vortex of cosmic consciousness. When people are able to perceive them as I did, they often take a form extracted from the human mind. We can see them in human form, but in essence they are only vortexes or energies. Let me describe what I saw. I was in my bedroom at night watching TV. I happened to look over to my right near my bed and saw this creature in the air. It was very small—around five feet tall. It had brown hair down to its shoulders and wore a wine-colored cloth. It looked straight ahead, and when I looked at it, the face turned into a smile. Its eyes and forehead looked like those of a medieval creature. It was there for an instant and then left. It communicated with me in my thoughts and left. I felt as though this creature had known me forever and knew all about me and my life. It then disappeared. I was on the radio, as a guest speaker, and there was a paranormal expert on the show. When I described this incident to him, he told me I had seen a deva. I must trust in his judgment and believe him. Why it appeared to me, I really do not know, but that evening I was on the phone with a psychic talking to him about contacting my angels, and when I hung up the phone, this entity appeared in my room. While talking to this psychic, I heard a noise in the office room, and I think it was this creature. These devas have memory and learn from past experiences. For example, a deva of the oak trees is interested only in the growth of oak trees, and a healing deva works only with healing energies. I believe that this was a healing deva and that it was trying to heal me after the death of my husband. Devas help people.

The nature spirits are devas, gnomes, kobolds, giants, mountain devas, nymphs, undines, nixies, elves or sylphs, fairies, storm devas, salamanders or fire spirits, fauns, Pan, werewolves, dragons, house spirits, birth fairies, guardian spirits, the jinn, and sound and dance spirits. You can learn more about these other types of spirits in other informative literature.

The classification of angels will now be listed:

1. The seraphim distribute the universal force that allows mankind to focus on the divine unity within themselves.
2. The cherubim regulate and equilibrate the primordial chaos. They provide us the forms by which we are able to visualize divine things. Their vibrations are seen in the form of light as well as sounds. Their function is to maintain manifestation in movement.
3. The thornes allow our spirit to focus the images formed by the cherubim.

4. The dominions are like a reservoir of energy that animates nature. They give to men the necessary force to conquer the inner enemy and to achieve the ends that are assigned to them. The dominions are angels of leadership. They regulate the duties of the angels, making known the commands of God.

5. The powers (seraphim) have to do with divine sanctity and purification. They fight against the evil spirits who attempt to wreak chaos through human beings.

6. The virtues are known as the spirits of motion and control the elements. They govern all nature.

7. The principalities embrace all forces.

8. The archangels rule over the animal kingdom and give man domination over it.

9. The angels (keroubim) are the guardians of the threshold. They defend the holiness of God against fallen men who would otherwise take the tree of life. They are the most caring, and assist those who ask for help.

I hope this little lesson will make all you readers interested in finding out more about these unique spirits that surround our world and beyond.

Now, getting back to ghosts and spirits, what they are and why they haunt us. They are souls who did not pass into the light or the next dimension when their physical bodies died here on Earth.

These spirits did not pass over for one of the following reasons:

1. They have unfinished business here on Earth.

2. They are afraid to move on to the next level because of what they think awaits them.
3. They want to pass over but cannot see the "light."
4. They like it here and just want to hang around us!

Entities can also be seen when they are in the form of residual energy. A certain spot or location (such as a house) holds the energy of past occupants and events, and anyone there at the right time and place can see a replay of certain events.

The word *poltergeists* also comes up in this discussion of spirits. These energies are *not* from a person who once lived on this Earth. Generally, poltergeists are not connected with the spirit of someone who has passed on. They are *not* ghosts. Poltergeist activity is really associated with children, adolescents, or people with emotional problems. A form of mind-over-matter energy is expended from the living person, creating loud noises and causing furniture to move around, objects to move up and down, and any type of strange, foul odors.

All these paranormal activities drain your health and energy. I have never experienced poltergeist activity in the house, but these apparitions, orbs, and spirit activity drain a person's health and energy. I am now going to church every Sunday. I heard a bang in my bedroom on New Year's Eve night and went to church New Year's Day for a Mass that the church was doing for my husband. I came home and the house was very quiet, as though whatever has been here had left—for a while, anyway. I will continue to go to church every Sunday and take my son.

Well, the paranormal activity stopped for one day and the next morning we saw an orb leave the house. This means it was here at night. So praying may help, but it does not seem to stop what is happening here. I will continue to go to church and see what happens.

I want to explain the difference between ghosts and spirits. Ghosts and spirits are energy from a life that previously existed on this Earth. Energy is the way in which ghosts and spirits can manifest themselves here on this Earth. Electricity is a conduit to allow spirits and ghosts to manifest themselves. Batteries can be drained when a ghost appears. Lights can dim or even be turned off as spirits enter this dimension. I always have the overhead light on in my bedroom at night when I sleep. I put the light on dim. One night, I fell asleep in my bedroom and woke up with the light off. I immediately jumped up and ran to the door, where the light switch is on the wall. As I jumped up and ran toward the door, an entity was standing there; I felt it as I ran to the door. I ran into it without knowing it was standing there. I heard a small crying out, and it moved toward the left side, away from the door. I put the light on again and knew there was something in my room watching me while I was asleep.

There is also something called emotional energy. A happy, positive person will give off good energy and enable a spirit (who has passed into the light) to come back and give messages to their loved ones. A ghost will feed off the negative energies of people, which is how they manifest themselves here on Earth.

Another type of energy is the energy of moving water. This energy from nature also allows spirits and ghosts to manifest themselves. An example of this happened when I was on a cruise ship. I was in my cabin lying down when my son and

I heard a spirit talk. She said "Bonjour" and touched my face. We also saw a manifestation of my husband in the cabin. He was standing near the desk. I fell asleep, and when I woke up, I saw a hand take the covers and cover me up with them and wave good-bye to me over and over again. It seemed as though I could not move for a moment. This was quite strange and scary for me. So, yes, moving water aids in the manifestation of spirits.

Heat is another type of energy for the manifestation of spirits and ghosts. In order for the ghosts and spirits to energize themselves and appear, they absorb heat energy. This, in turn, slows the movement of the molecules. This creates a cooling effect and produces "cold spots" in the room. That is why when a ghost or spirit appears in the room, the room gets cold. It tells us that at this particular area, a ghost or spirit is trying to manifest itself or has manifested itself in this area.

Just remember that when the body dies, the spirit lives on in another state, with all memories, personality traits, and intelligence intact, and that the spirit world is in fact all around us occupying space at a vibrational speed that is different from physical matter here.

Everything that is living (dead or inanimate) has a vibrational speed; again, that is a basic law of physics.

When we die, that conscious being now changes form. The part of us that is consciousness changes form when the life supporting it ceases.

When a medium communicates with a spirit, the spirit often presents itself as it was remembered here on the physical plane. This means that the medium can describe the person as they remember themselves, for example, as tall, with blue eyes, blond hair, any distinguishing features, and so on; the person's personality and character; any illnesses or complaints they had; how they died; life experiences; and more. That is why, when my husband returns here, I can sometimes hear a heavy breathing as though that is what he sounded like when he was dying. He died of a heart attack on February 7, 2005.

The description of how the spirit looked when they were on this Earth is what the spirit remembers about their life, but it is not how they actually are now, since they no longer occupy the physical plane. They simply remember what they looked like, and re-create it at will for whatever purpose. It could be a haunting or it could be so that a medium can pass on the information to help their loved ones recognize them during a sitting. As I told you before, spirits are very powerful. They can manifest themselves at will, haunt, talk, and deliver messages to their loved ones.

The next chapter will be on orbs, which is how a spirit travels from plane to plane.

CHAPTER 4

ORBS

When orbs are present, it means they are trying to communicate with the physical world. Capturing an orb in a photo, on a video camera, or on a camcorder is a genuine sign of spirit energy being present at that time. As I have found out in my experiences with orbs, spirit orb activity is not visible to the naked eye. You could be standing right next to an orb and not see it with the naked eye. I documented this when orbs were picked up on my video camera when I was in my living room. I could not see anything with my naked eye, but on the video camera, I saw orbs with a nucleus inside. A nucleus is the spirit inside the orb. I could see a head and a body in the orb. I have this picture in the book, and you can see for yourself the results of the camera picking up the images of the orbs. True spirit orbs tend to appear to have faces, or other patterns in the orbs, and as I mentioned, they have a nucleus of some kind. The orb captured in my living room in January 2012 had the face of my husband. I took a magnifying glass and could see his face in the orb along with a bright light coming down in the living room and a rod-shaped white light coming down with the light at the same time the orb appeared. As the orb left, the light left. It was a very, very exciting thing to see.

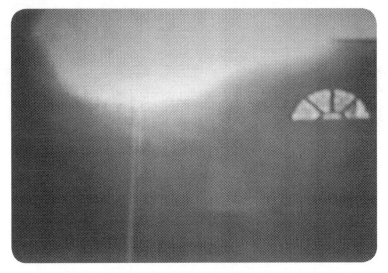

ROD OF LIGHT IN LIVING ROOM

Orbs are sometimes accompanied by delicate mists or smoky wisps as the physical apparition is attempted and progresses. I have these mists on my camera along with the orbs. If you look closely, these mists can show the actual shape and form of the person manifesting. It takes a tremendous amount of energy for a spirit to materialize here in our environment. Spirits aren't often successful at fully materializing, but more often than not, they can create either an intentional or unintentional reaction of some kind that we can sense, such as an orb or a noise, to prove that they are there. I have experienced bangs on the wall, cabinets opening in the kitchen, and even my husband's voice talking to me. Never in a million years did I think that was possible. To hear the voice of my husband as though he is right there even though I can't see him is unbelievable. That is why I wrote my first book, *You Can't Control the Soul,* and why I am writing this second book.

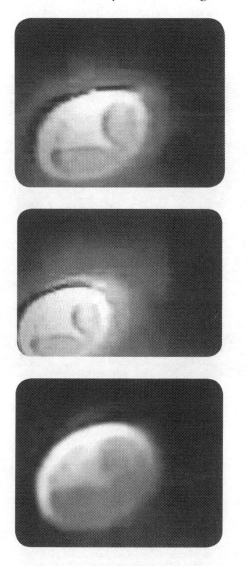

ORB WITH SPIRIT IN IT

Let's get back to discussing orbs. A spirit is represented in an orb configuration pattern as seen in the pictures from my video camera. When a spirit is moving about, its shape is an orb with a contrail (vapor), but when it is at rest, meaning no longer in motion, the spirit energy expands into an ecto-vapor or ectoplasm.

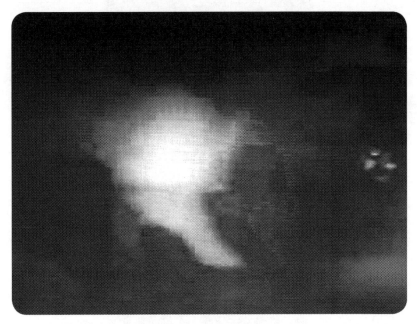

ORB WITH CONTRAIL

Often as you can see in my orb pictures, an orb will contain more than one soul, and when its spirit energy is released, multiple orbs flow forth from a single orb. An orb may be observed as a small white ball of light shooting through the room, as seen in my pictures. It will go through a wall into a room. The so-called orb theory is explained as a spiritual orb representing the soul of a departed person. The soul is the essence of who they were in life, complete with their intelligence, their emotions, and their personality. This symbol of an orb circle represents external existence, with no beginning and no end.

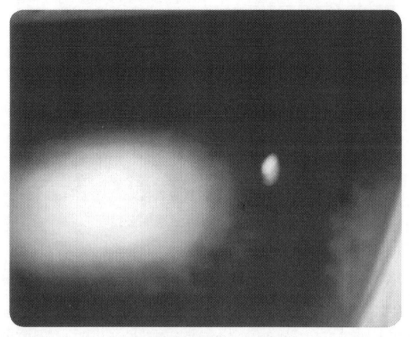

CLUSTER OF ORBS

Spirits are not always successful at manifesting fully. They can create an intentional or unintentional reaction of some kind that we are able to sense, such as these orbs of light, or a noise such as a knock on the wall to prove to us they are there. I often hear some type of electrical static telling me that there is a spirit present. I hear this noise in my bedroom at night when I am trying to sleep. I turn around from my pillow and look to see if anything is there. I know they are there but cannot see them. They sometimes materialize near my bed when I wake up. One night I woke up and a woman was lying near me in my bed. The woman had blond hair and it looked strange, as though it was an artificial person lying there. I jumped up and the entity was gone.

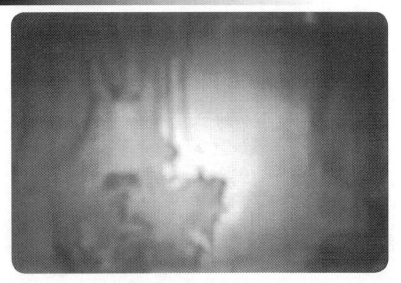

SPIRIT ENTERING HOUSE

The orbs enter the house in the morning when I leave for work. I saw four orbs fly into the house just last week, on February 29, 2012. When there is an upset here in the house, they come. My son heard them talking in his room as he was sleeping one day. I asked him, "What did you hear?" He said he heard only muttering but could not hear what they were saying.

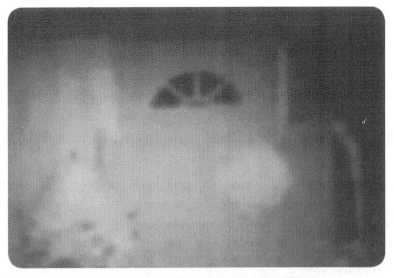

FLYING ORB ENTERING HOUSE

A strange occurrence happened here again the week of March 20, 2012. I had a very restless evening trying to fall asleep. I kept getting up and finally went downstairs to the kitchen for a Coke. I finally fell asleep but felt a pulling of my body to the other side of the bed. It felt like there was someone next to me in the bed and I was trying to talk to him or her. I felt it was my husband's soul, but as I moved, there was someone there with long hair flowing into my face. I then saw myself downstairs in the living room. Two spirits materialized, standing near the lamp by the door. One of them passed by me and went into the kitchen. One was looking at me and smiling, and when he approached me, he had a terrible smell to him. It smelled like death—a corpse. They started up the stairs to my room, and I was yelling at them not to go up there. When I told my son about this dream, he looked at the camera that night and saw a gigantic orb outside the house. These life forms travel in groups. These spirits at times do not want to move to the next level of existence. When they stay behind, they are obsessed in some way with their previous life and become similar to a psychotic human being. I feel that my husband has become very, very crazy for this reason. He continues to either stay here or keep coming back day after day. He brings others in these gigantic orbs with him to this house. The longer these spirits stay behind, the more difficult it will be for them to find their way to the next level, which is the spirit world.

I have captured these ghostly orbs on camera. They can be completely transparent or display themselves like the photographs I have in a bright, solid form. It is theorized that these ghosts prefer the form of an orb (ball of light) because it takes much less energy than any other form and thus is the mode of choice for these ghosts. I have also noted that when the weather is cold, there is more paranormal activity here than in the hotter months. I wondered why this would be. I found out that there is more static electricity in the atmosphere between October and February.

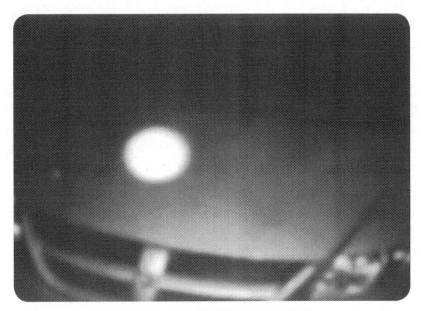

ORB OUTSIDE THE HOUSE

I saw my husband's face turning in the orb that appeared in my living room in January 2012. There was a strange rod of light outside the house at the same time the orb appeared. I have a picture of this rod in my book. It is called an "energy line," which the spirits in orbs travel down until reaching their desired destination. These orbs are dimensional orbs that open up to the other dimension. My son keeps telling me how his astral body goes to the other side at night. He is in a dark place. He asks these spirits, "Where is my father?" and one of them points across the room. My husband is with another person and starts to talk to my son. The last communication with my husband was him telling my son, "You think you can have your cake and eat it, too? You and your mother will not have any peace until we get out of this place and get to heaven." He wants us to keep praying for him. The prayers that were already said for him were not enough. This message to my son I believe was true. My son has also been telling me of orbs entering the house when I leave and his room being haunted as he takes a nap during the day. He has seen an entity enter his room through the wall. It was telling him something about Jesus, but he could not hear what it said. The spirits seem to connect with my son more than they do me. I would just get mad and tell them to get out. My son sees fingerprints in his room as though someone is touching his CDs, tapes, and records. They seem to be very interested in who comes over to the house and what objects are in the house.

CHAPTER 5

THE SHADOW PEOPLE

Watch out for the shadow people. They are lurking around corners. I have seen a shadow person hiding around the corner in my kitchen!

As I was preparing to go on a cruise, I was sitting in my dining room writing out checks to be mailed before I left. I heard a noise in my living room, which connects to the dining room. The kitchen is an open area with no door. As I proceeded to get up to see what the noise was in the living room, I started to go into the kitchen first and saw a shadow person hiding around the corner by the wall. It actually looked like a silhouette of my husband. It saw me and immediately disappeared. I was in shock to see such a strange, scary apparition. I immediately left the dining room and went up to my bedroom. I could not wait to get out of this house and go on my cruise. This phenomenon of the shadow people seems to be on the rise around the world based on numerous sightings with greater frequency. These beings are shaped like humans, but they have no real body. They are merely shadows lurking in various places. Did you ever notice a strange shadow that seemed out of place? It's possible you were witnessing a shadow person! When you do see a shadow person, they usually disappear. Some theories suggest that these shadow people are from another world/universe. Do they come here to check on us for some reason? They may be just curious about this world or us. I think they are ghosts and can appear as shadow people along with appearing as orbs. Of course, shadow people have never talked to us, so they will continue to be a mystery among us. Yet, with all my experiences with the paranormal, I am 95 percent sure that a shadow person is a spirit coming back. It is *not* an alien or some other strange creature. It is the spirit of a dead person coming back, and nothing else! A couple of months ago, in July 2012, I woke up and saw a shadow person standing near my bed. The outline looked like my husband, and I was just about to scream when it moved over to the front of my bed where I was sleeping and disappeared near the head of the bed. This was my husband again, watching me or looking at me while I slept. He is concerned about me and wants to make sure I am okay.

I have collected some data on their appearances. They range in height from four to eight feet. They can be seen in various levels of transparency. They range in levels of darkness. I saw one shadow person on my stairs who was the blackest black

I have ever seen. The shadow person in my kitchen was less black than the one on the stairs. Some of these shadow people are solid black forms and not completely transparent. They can be male or female. I have seen only males. If you see one straight on, they are called "free standers," which is what I saw on the stairs. They are seen where there is paranormal activity. I have been told that sightings of these free standers are quite rare, but I have seen them in my home. They may also be noticed by footsteps. My son hears footsteps going up the stairs to my bedroom when he is downstairs. This happens only when I am not at home. The so-called Hat Man, which is a variation of a shadow person, who is mostly featureless, have masculine forms and wear old fashioned hats. This image was seen in shadow form near my bed. I woke up and saw it staring at me and then it disappeared. The funny part of this is that the face looked like my husband's face!

There is another theory about "The Old Woman" shadow person. She is usually around when a victim is in sleep paralysis. She is associated with fear and bad dreams. She is associated with being held down, unable to move, and being drained. This has happened to me in the last month. I was sleeping and remember being pulled to the opposite side of the bed, where there was some type of entity lying next to me. I tried to talk, but I was paralyzed. I felt my body being pulled to the other side of the bed, and then I felt long hair in my face. I remember trying to brush the hair out of my face, and then I found myself downstairs, where I noticed two men near the lamp in my living room. They were looking at me, and one walked toward me. I smelled a terrible odor as he walked over to me—like a decayed body. He was wearing a tan jacket and smiling at me. He did not say anything to me. Another man walked by me and walked into my kitchen while holding an object. It looked like a silver object with a hole in the middle of it like an upside-down shade you put on a lamp, but it was all metal with a silver color. This man then started to go upstairs to my room, and I remember yelling at him, "Don't go up there!" I don't remember anything else about that night, but I do remember I was quite stressed and could not fall asleep until about 2:00 a.m. This is when sleep paralysis occurs—when the body falls asleep and the mind is still awake.

Some theories about shadow people say they are ghosts from purgatory. I think that the spirits coming to this house are in purgatory. My son was sleeping and told me he heard my husband talking to him in his sleep. My husband asked my son, "Do you think you and your mother can have your cake and eat it, too? Well, while we are here in this place, we will continue to bother you and your mother until we can get out of here." Now, I believe this message. I have had prayers said for my husband at church and given money to a group of monks who pray for the departed for thirty days. A Mass is said for the departed every day for thirty days. The hauntings still continue here!

These shadow people are disembodied humans who are lost. They have not gone forward in life's journey but are refusing to go toward the light after the death of their physical body. These shadow people are thus not devils, demons, or aliens, as some people may believe. They are really trapped by their minds and seem to be reliving their former lives. They remain as earthbound spirits.

The personalities of shadow people can vary from nice to nasty—not any different from people you meet who are still in bodies. My husband comes back as a shadow person, and I heard his voice being very angry one night as I was upstairs in my bedroom watching television. This was just after my first book was released. I had put some negative things about my husband in the book, which is titled *You Can't Control the Soul* and is on Amazon.com and Barnes and Noble.com. I was watching TV when I heard my husband call my name downstairs in an angry way. I got very scared and upset when I heard his voice. He yelled out "Diana" very loudly and sounded as if he was very mad. I believe his personality has not changed as a spirit entity. When a person dies, their mental and physical condition will *not* change until they move into the light with loved ones, as a life-review or cleansing process occurs. After the life review, the spirits become "clean" as misthinking is purged and truth and understanding is gained. Shadow people are considered "unclean" spirits, and retain their emotional and physical baggage. This manifests as a distinct personality, mentality, aliment, pain, appearance, or something else—even an odor. I smelled my husband's colostomy bag when he first died. We used to smell this odor from time to time around the house. They are trapped in their former state, and do not appear to advance in age, intellect, or any aspect of their condition until they choose to turn to loved ones who are with them, who are attempting to bring them forward into the light and life.

Some people believe that shadow people may be the extra-dimensional inhabitants of another universe. This phenomenon of the shadow people seems to be on the rise around the world. There appears to be more sightings, with greater frequency.

In Japanese forklore, a ghost is called a *yurei*. According to the Japanese, all humans have a spirit or soul called a *reikon*. When a person dies, the reikon leaves the body and enters a form of purgatory, where it waits for the proper funeral and post-funeral rites to be performed, so that it may join its ancestors. However, if the person dies in a sudden or violent manner, such as by murder or suicide, and the proper rites have not been performed, or if they are influenced by some powerful emotions such as desire for some type of revenge, love, jealousy, hatred, or sorrow, the reikon is thought to transform into a yurei, which can then bridge the gap back to the physical world. The yurei exists on Earth until it can be laid to rest, either by performing the missing rituals or resolving the emotional conflicts that still tie it to the physical plane. If the rituals are not completed or the conflict is left unresolved, the yurei will persist in its hauntings. This is what is happening here in my house. These emotional conflicts that my husband has taken with him to the other dimension are the reason he continues to haunt my son and me. In Japanese culture, my husband would be called an *onryo,* which is a vengeful ghost who comes back from purgatory for a wrong done to them during their lifetime. The yurei do not wander randomly, but generally stay near a specific location, such as where they were killed or where their body lies, or they follow a specific person, such as their murderer or a beloved. They usually appear between 2:00 and 3:00 a.m., which is called the witching hour for Japan, when the veils between the world of the dead and the world of the living are at their thinnest.

The yurei will continue to haunt that particular person or place until their purpose is fulfilled and they can move on to the afterlife.

While writing this book, I encountered another shadow person in my bedroom. It was June 9, 2012, which was my wedding anniversary. I woke up around 3:00 a.m. and saw a man in shadow form looking at me. The figure walked around to my bed and then disappeared. I was just about to scream, but it left. I believe this was my husband watching me. It was our thirty-fourth wedding anniversary. I believe the dead remember their former life and watch and protect their loved ones here on Earth.

Chapter 6

Astral Projection

What is astral projection? Many people have never heard of this term. There are people who do not believe that your soul can go to the astral plane (astral world) at night while you are sleeping. This astral plane is the world of the planetary spheres, crossed by the soul in its astral body on the way to being born and after death, and it is generally populated by angels, spirits, and other immaterial beings.

According to Wikipedia, "astral projection (or astral travel) is an interpretation of out-of-body experience (OBE) that assumes the existence of an 'astral body' separate from the physical body and capable of traveling outside it. Astral projection or travel denotes the astral body leaving the physical body to travel in the astral plane." Astral projection from Webster's New Millennium Dictionary of English, Preview Edition (v0.9.7) Retrieved June 21, 2008, from Dictionary.com website.

One night about three years ago, I was in my bedroom just lying down but not asleep yet. I felt upset that my husband was not here anymore and finally fell asleep. I found myself downstairs in the living room but up in the air. I was near the curtains in the living room, and my body was swaying back and forth while the curtains moved as though there was a great wind there. This swaying was my astral body. According to the book by Sylvan Muldoon and Hereward Carrington called *The Projection of the Astral Body* the astral body sways back and forth, which is what I experienced in my living room. I remember calling my husband's name—"Brad, Brad"—but my voice was different; it was much weaker, as though I could hardly talk. I then remember flying through the door to the downstairs and seeing my husband with other people. I believe this was my astral body going to the other side. As your body lies in a sleep state, your astral body travels to other dimensions. It is connected with a cord about the size of a silver dollar and is attached to your physical body in the middle of the forehead. This astral cable is an elastic-type structure, connecting the astral body to the physical. According to Muldoon and Carrington, the less space that lies between the two bodies, the greater the thickness of the astral cable, the greater its magnetic pull and the more difficult it is to hold the stability of the phantom. The phantom is your physical body in sleep state.

My son has seen his astral body in his mirror downstairs in his bedroom. He saw his astral body as a mist and could see some facial features. He saw the cord connected to his physical body as his body was in bed. The cord definitely comes out of the middle of the forehead. He felt himself going into a vortex and spinning until he was able to get out. He told me when he woke up that he had a very bad headache.

The more energy condensed in the astral body, the more tightly that body will be bound to the physical body. If the person becomes weakened to a great extent, probably from illness, the astral body cannot remain in the physical at all and moves out, sometimes permanently. My husband told me two weeks before he died that he was flying around the bedroom one night and saw me sleeping in the bed. This was his astral body wanting to get out of his physical body. He died two weeks later.

Your astral body is the "real" you! It is the astral entity that is the real you. This astral body is the universal energy that is the breath of life.

Another good book on astral projection is *Leaving the Body* written by D. Scott Rogo. He says that "astral projection is the ability to leave the body at will." He talks about the techniques needed to have an OBE. The book talks about the hypnagogic state, which is the curious state between waking and sleeping. This is a borderline sleeping state that can induce astral projection. The projection of the astral body will be more successful if it is done in the hypnagogic state, when coming out of sleep. When a person awakes in this so-called "nocturnal paralysis," which was written about in *The Projection of the Astral Body,* we become alarmed.

The person wants to become physically active again and struggles with himself to be free. This is a condition that I have experienced time and again while I was in some type of hypnagogic state. I woke up in my bed facing the pillow. I felt a gigantic pressure on top of me and pushing into me. I grew alarmed and thought in my conscious mind that someone was trying to kill me. I felt a tremendous pushing on my back, as though someone was trying to push into me. I tried to reach for the phone but was in this nocturnal paralysis. This astral catalepsy called "nocturnal paralysis" is definitely real. I have experienced it and have to tell all of you that this truly exists. This catalepsy is more likely to occur from the sleeping state to the waking than the reverse. I am totally convinced that this state occurs in many astral projections when the astral body returns to the physical world.

This condition of nocturnal paralysis finally stopped when I was able to reach the phone and the pushing on top of my back stopped. The astral body returned to the physical body and then I woke up. It was quite a scary experience. I am truly convinced that the other souls induce my son and I to go into astral projection. When we hear movement or sound in the house, especially in the bedroom or downstairs in the living room, we astral-project that evening. My son just told me about another experience that happened May 14, 2012. I came home and my son told me he was taking a nap downstairs in his bedroom and saw my husband in his astral travels. He said my husband was sitting at a table in the other world. There was a girl there also, playing an instrument. She spoke to my son and said, "Did you die?" He said no and he was floating above her in the other world. My husband was sitting in some room and told the girl—"No, I am not going to let him alone. He owes me." Then my son felt himself swirling around and around and finally felt himself back in his room. He felt very upset over this experience. I believe it happened. A very upsetting situation continues here, and I will eventually have a psychic come over to see what is really happening here.

Let's continue to talk about astral projection, what it really is, and how people go to different planes while in their astral bodies. This hypnagogic state is the state between half waking and half sleeping that lasts about a few minutes or may be prolonged for at least fifteen minutes when you experience that sensation of "falling." As sleep is coming on, you experience this sensation of falling. Fatigue, general ill health, or nervousness will provoke this condition. You may become conscious, but your motor centers may awaken more slowly, and this produces sleep paralysis. Sleep paralysis really scares many people as they experience this strange phenomenon. I wake up in the middle of the night and see apparitions in my home but have this sleep paralysis and cannot move when they are in the room. I then awake fully and the apparitions are gone. I feel extremely terrified by these strange experiences. This has happened quite a lot since the death of my husband, and I find the experience quite scary. It's almost unbelievable to see the dead in my room trying to communicate with me.

When we astral-project, our thoughts control where we go and what we see in teleporting to different dimensional planes. During these lucid dreams and out-of-body experiences in astral projection, your thoughts guide your experience. When I saw my husband that night, I astral-projected to another dimension. I saw my husband sitting in a chair and bent down to kiss him. These were my thoughts—to see him again and contact him. If you are thinking about a friend, you will be in his or her house as you astral-project. Of course, astral projection could also backfire on you. You could contact the dead as you astral-project and become terrified. A woman named Erin Pavlina had a terrifying experience. She was in sleep paralysis and sensed three other entities in her bedroom, trying to coax her out of her body. She had problems trying to breathe, scream, and free herself from the paralysis. The more she fought it, the more terrified she became, until she eventually woke up and had a nervous breakdown. She thought these entities were in her room, talking about her and trying to pull her out of her body. The experience terrified her. She found many negative entities in the spirit world and learned to fight them.

Erin Pavlina is now a psychic medium and teaches others about her experience with astral projection. She says, "The body does not want to let go of the spirit, so it hangs on pretty tight. To overcome that tether, you're going to have a pretty strong reason for getting out. I don't recommend toying with astral projection. It's not necessary to astral project to live a proper life. However, I completely understand the thrill of it, so project safely if you're going to do it." So I leave it up to all of you as you read this book to astral-project or not. (Erin Pavlina's Blog interview January 7, 1985).

I must also talk about the laws of physics and astral projection. Science dismisses astral projection as being impossible according to the laws of physics. Science believes these experiences with so-called astral projection are flights of imagination, dreams, or hallucinations. According to studies on astral projection, at least 14 percent of the population has experienced astral projection or an OBE. Sometimes these astral projections occur during some type of crisis or emotional upset. I have experienced my astral projections when I am upset and miss my husband. It seems like the soul wants to find him and goes to another plane where the dead exist.

A common example involves near-fatal accidents, where the person later reports floating above their body near the ceiling in the hospital, watching as an observer, taking in action and conversations of the medical personnel working "below" them.

When people recover from these instances, they report watching their doctors pronounce them dead or call for a specific lifesaving technique later recounted and verified by those present. When astral projection occurs under these circumstances, it is referred to as a near-death experience (NDE).

CHAPTER 7

APPARITIONS

What are apparitions? The word *apparition* comes from the Latin *apparitio,* which means "appearance." An apparition is the spirit of a human or animal becoming visible to the eyes. Apparitions are often described as looking solid in appearance, though sometimes they are visibly "see-through." Occasionally, a full-body apparition is witnessed, whereas at other times only a part of the person or animal's spirit is seen, such as the upper body, the face, an arm, a hand, or even a foot.

Apparitions of the dead or dying may appear during the dying process or soon after death, or be seen repeatedly over years. Apparitions of the dead sometimes appear as a plea for help, to complete unfinished business, or as a farewell. You may also hear a voice giving messages to the living.

I have seen many apparitions in my home. The first one was of my husband standing in the window of my bedroom. I came home from work one night and happened to look up at my window and see the figure of my husband standing there. He looked as if he was thirty years old and was dressed all in black. He looked at me with no expression on his face. Then he disappeared. I had to go into that house all alone and was scared to death that night.

I have also seen apparitions of others in my bedroom. One night, I fell asleep in my bed. I awoke around 11:30 p.m., happened to look at the mirror, and saw a man standing by my bedroom door. I turned around and this man smiled at me, which made me start screaming. These apparitions look *real*! They actually look as if a real person is standing there. This man looked around forty-five years old and had curly, grayish hair. I did not recognize him, and I think he was one of the dead accompanying my husband as he came back.

Another time, I awoke in my bedroom and saw a young man standing near my bed holding a letter and smiling before he disappeared. I felt paralyzed and could not move when I saw this person. These are very terrifying appearances for me to witness. I don't like the idea that the dead come here and try to communicate with me.

The deliberate attempt to contact a spirit of a deceased person is known as necromancy, or in spiritism as a séance. I have never experienced a séance, nor do I want to participate in one.

I have heard my husband's voice about three times since his death. The first time was around 10:00 p.m. one night. I was alone in the house. I went to bed, turned the lights off, and just lay in bed, and then I heard his voice. It sounded as if my husband was right in the room with me near the front of the bed. He said, "I love you, Spitty." Spitty was his nickname for me, and it sounded as if he just wanted to let me know that love never dies, even after death.

These manifestations of the dead continue here in this house. Apparitions have also appeared downstairs in the living room and can appear or disappear in enclosed rooms. I have seen a woman pass through the living room wall and then disappear.

Let's discuss the different types of apparitions. First, there is the misty or translucent appearance that I have captured on my video camera. When orbs are present, a mist fills the room in which they appear. I have seen a face in this mist but the apparition did not appear.

The second type of manifestation is a solid-appearing person that is very lifelike. These apparitions can actually be mistaken for a real person. As they manifest into solid form, they can cast shadows and reflections.

Another type of manifestation is when the dead appear as a living person. I saw an apparition look exactly like my son in his downstairs living room. I happened to go downstairs to talk to my son, and before I got to his bedroom, I saw an apparition of him sitting on the living room floor. It smiled at me and immediately disappeared.

The majority of apparitions are witnessed by one person. There are cases when two people were in the same location, and one person could see the apparition and the other could not.

Apparitions of the dead tend to be seen in places where they used to live or even work. They appear to people they knew in life. According to Dr. Ian Stevenson (1982), "No fewer than 78% of apparitions of the dead were perceived by a [witness] to whom the [deceased person] had a strong emotional ties, such as a husband, wife or fiancé; and among apparitions of the living the percentage of such appearances rose even higher, to 92%."(Stevenson I. (1982). The Contribution of Apparitions to the Evidence of Survival. Journal of the American Society for Psychical Research, 76, 341-358.)

I have also noticed that the farther one gets from a person's time of death, the less frequently that person's apparition appears. These solid apparitions appeared the first year after my husband's death. I have not seen a solid-appearing apparition for about two years now. I see only shadows and orbs now and *not* solid-appearing apparitions, which I am quite relieved about. There is nothing more scary than seeing a dead person appear like a real-life human being. I feel as if they will want to touch me or talk to me. This scares me to death!

Sometimes the appearance of these apparitions is accompanied by feelings of cold, wind, or a touch. I felt a hand touch my face two years ago when I was recovering from the shingles. I got these terrible shingles on the right side of my face. I woke up one morning with a rash and blisters on my face. This was accompanied by the symptoms of a cold. I immediately went to my doctor on Monday morning, and he told me I had shingles and gave me a medication. After about four days, I experienced burning and pain on the right side of my face. One night, I was just lying down in my bed and felt a hand touch my face twice. It was trying to comfort me. About one week later, the shingles disappeared without any permanent damage. Thank God!

I have also had auditory apparitional experiences. I have heard the sound of my husband's voice in my bedroom and downstairs in the living room. It sounded as though he was alive and just standing near me.

Of course, the rarest apparition is a full-body apparition. These apparitions are intelligent ghosts. The difference between a haunting and these apparitions is that the latter have intelligence. According to a "survival theory," these are the parts of the human that survive the death of the physical body. These apparitions can and will appear to the living while they are awake, sleeping, or in an altered state of consciousness. The majority of my experiences with apparitions happened when I was in an altered state of consciousness.

I will now discuss three types of visions.

The first type of vision is called a corporeal vision. Corporeal visions are supernatural manifestations of an object to the eyes of the body. You can call seeing the unresurrected dead or pure spirit a corporeal vision.

The second type of vision is called an imaginative vision.

The object exists only in the person's imagination. This is the case in a supernatural hallucination. Imaginative apparitions are of short duration. It is often difficult to decide whether a vision is corporeal or imaginative.

The third type of vision is called an intellectual vision. Intellectual visions perceive the object without a sensible image. Intellectual visions are of a supernatural order. They take place in the pure understanding of what you are seeing. These intellectual visions are mostly of the divine experience.

There are different types of apparitions, as discussed above—the first being residual haunting. These residual haunts are not apparitions of ghosts but the energy and the habits of spirits remaining in specific areas. After my husband died, he came into my bedroom and put a drink down on the dresser. He used to drink rum and Coke when he was alive. I could hear the ice cubes moving around in the glass. This is how ghosts make themselves known—through sounds. These hauntings are generally not thought of as spirits, but are the energy of the people who have passed on—the energy of the spirit.

I want to discuss poltergeists in this book. The word *poltergeist* comes from the German words for "noisy spirits." Poltergeists are often spirits that combine different actions over time. They interact by moving objects, throwing objects, screaming, banging objects, and opening and closing objects. I have experienced the throwing of an object in my bedroom. I had a plaque on the wall that said "God Bless This Home." I woke up in the middle of the night and saw the plaque come off the wall and get thrown near my bed. It did not hit me but was thrown next to me. I have also experienced the kitchen cabinets being opened right in front of me. Sometimes, when my son or I are upset, these particular hauntings will appear. I think these types of haunting feed off people's negative emotions.

Another type of apparition is called a demonic apparition. These are inhuman appearances and powers among humans. These types of demonic spirits *must* be avoided. They are superhuman. They are very strong and forceful. They can attack, injure, appear, and speak to people. They are known to fly, disappear, and do whatever they wish to do. No type of scientific investigation can assist with demonic possession or activity.

Another type of apparition, as I discussed in a previous chapter, is the shadow people. Shadow people appear at times as a silhouette of a person—usually male, but lacking any gender characteristics. I saw a silhouette of a man in my bedroom just a few days ago. I could see the head, which looked like that of a man, above a body that was quite large. It moved fast and then just disappeared. Shadow people will dart behind walls, into closets, and behind television sets, bushes, and buildings. The most common characteristic of these shadow people is that they are intensely dark.

Apparitions called crisis apparitions are of the dying or recently dead. They appear to people with whom they have close emotional ties in onetime visits either at the time of death or while they are dying. This encounter is usually a farewell.

Another type of apparition is called a benevolent apparition, which has a protective nature. The benevolent entity is a loved one and is looking to protect a loved one against a demon or other possibly violent entity. I know that when I have trouble at work or am upset, the ghosts appear and come back to this house. They may also get upset and appear here.

An apparition is called a malevolent apparition when a ghost or demon is trying to inflict some type of harm on the living. The entity is angry about events that occurred in its life, is jealous of the living, or is a malicious personality in general; the entity seeks attention or is defensive of its home and wants the current residents to depart, or sad and wants others to acknowledge its sadness and feel its misery. Demons can be present when a murder occurred in the area.

The next type of apparition is called a benign apparition, which is an intelligent or residual haunting.

Conclusions about the above apparitions are as follows:

Apparitions make one or several visits to someone (they may or may not have known the person while alive).

There are apparitions that linger for months or years around a particular location or person that they loved or associated with when alive. This is the case in my house. My husband continues to haunt and appear in different manifestations in this house. He returns as a dark shadow, an orb, or a full-bodied apparition. Quite scary stuff.

I have also seen apparitions downstairs in my living room and in my bedroom. This happened with astral projection. My astral body sees these apparitions, not my physical body. I woke up years ago to see two people in my bedroom. My body was asleep, but my astral body saw these people—a man and a woman standing in my bedroom. The man was bald with a white shirt and black pants. The woman had long black hair and smiled at me. She did not say anything to me, but the man did. He asked me, "Do you want to go with us?" I said no, I could not. "I have to stay here and take care of my son," I said. I asked this man, "Who determines this?" He answered, "God—God does." I saw the bedroom door open and there was a light in the hallway. The light turned into my husband, and he was facing the wall. He said, "I can't talk to you now; I am busy doing something." Very strange, scary apparitions.

The Egyptian *Book of the Dead* shows deceased people in the afterlife appearing much as they did before death, including the style of dress. My son tells me that when he astral-projects to the other side, he sees my husband as he looked in life. His hair is combed the same way, and his style of dress is the same. The house or place where my husband is looks like my home, with some exceptions. According to ancient Egyptian history, the dead travel to the netherworld, where they are assigned a position and lead an existence similar in some ways to that of the living. I truly believe this, as my son has seen my husband in the other dimension doing different things.

People who experience apparitions are by no means always frightened by it. They may feel soothed or reassured at times of crisis or ongoing stress in their lives. When I was in bed years ago, I heard my husband's voice tell me, "I love you, Spitty." Spitty was the name my husband always called me when he was alive. I did get rather scared, because I was alone in the house. I proceeded to go downstairs to get out of the bedroom and saw my husband's face move across the fireplace. He was laughing! I called my son and told him about this experience, and he was very concerned that I was there alone. Obviously, I could not sleep that night.

The orb that I captured in the house had a spirit in it. I took a magnifying glass and looked at the orb and at the person inside it. It looked like my husband, with his black hair and the shape of his head. He looked young, as he had looked when he was around thirty to thirty-five years old. I could not believe such a thing. A person can die but come back traveling in an orb! Unbelievable.

There are so many things about death and spirits we do not know. There should be a committee initiated by the government to really study the paranormal and detect what is real and what is not. We are all interested is what happens after death, and the government should have committees set up to study it. I think we would all benefit by finding out what we can do to communicate with the dead, and how they can inform us of their powers and where they go after physical death.

Another strange occurrence started in July 2012. I have been hearing whistling in my room. I wake up and can hear some spirit whistle near the dresser and then stop. Once, I got up and put the light on and got really mad. I told this spirit, "Get out right now. This is my house, and I do not want you here." Who knows how long it will last. They will be coming back as strong as ever when the weather gets cold. There is not much paranormal activity when the weather is very warm. Why this is the case, I am not sure yet. It probably has to do with the cold weather increasing the electromagnetic activity in the air.

CHAPTER 8

HEAVEN

Is heaven real? Of course it is! Do not doubt this for a moment. I know my husband is in heaven, because an apparition of an angel told me.

About six months ago, I was talking to my son about heaven. "Is Daddy in heaven?" my son asked. Well, I thought about it and remembered when he first died. I was in my bed lying down when I heard chimes coming from the ceiling near the bedroom window. I saw a shadow come down at the same time I heard the chimes. The music lasted about one second, and then the shadow walked over to my nightstand and looked at a picture I had of my husband, son, and me on a cruise ship. I could see the shadow's arms. It actually looked like my husband but in shadow form. I did not get scared but stared in disbelief that I could see such a thing and that this was real. I continued to watch and stayed very quiet and did not move. The shadow looked directly at the picture of me and my son. It really was staring at my picture as though it wanted to remember me. It then just disappeared into thin air. So, remembering this experience, I told my son, "Yes, your father is in heaven." I also know there are angels in this house listening to our conversations. As I was going upstairs to my bedroom one night, I happened to see a person standing near my bed. It was a girl about two feet tall. She was very pretty. She had black hair, which was a couple of inches down from her ears. She pointed to the ceiling as if to say, "Your husband is up in heaven."

In heaven, there is no more death or mourning or crying or pain. The old order of the way things were has passed away. In the Bible it says, "The new Jerusalem will be the external home of God's people." Of this place, the Bible says that "nothing unclean and no one who practices abomination and lying, shall ever come into it, but only those whose names are written in [Jesus'] book of life" (Revelation 21:27).

We are told that all people will undergo a bodily resurrection from the dead, and all will appear before the judgment seat of Christ (Revelation 20:11-13). Though Jesus initially came to Earth as a savior, He will now sit as judge. Those whose names are not found written in his book of life will be cast into the lake of fire (Revelation 20:14-15).

Some people have the idea that everyone will go to heaven, which is not the case. Jesus said that only those who believe in Him would find life, because "no one comes to the Father except through Me" (John 14:6). In Revelation 7:9 we are told that in heaven, there will be a multitude of people from every tribe, language, people, and nation who will have external life because of their faith in Jesus. Those who have rejected God will not be with Him.

Yes, this is really true. I am a Roman Catholic, and I truly believe the above statements from the Bible.

Yes, there is external life. Yes, your soul continues to exist when your physical body dies. Heaven is beautiful, with beautiful flowers and beautiful music. I was blessed to hear this music for one second. It was the most exquisite music I had ever heard. It is hard to describe it, though. It sounded like chimes and harps. I heard it for only an instant, and that was that. Heaven opened up to let my husband come down for a few minutes. He then went back. In my experiences with the afterlife, I can see my husband with other people. My mother-in-law is also in heaven, as I saw her there. She was a young woman again. She was a redhead and was talking to me, and then all of a sudden she turned around to see someone. I could not see who it was, and then I returned to my physical body. The astral body was up in heaven. I also saw images of my mother and father. I saw my mother smile at me, and my father's face was right in front of me. I loved them very much, and I felt good after seeing them again even for a brief moment.

When my husband first died, I contacted a medium about him and my mother. The medium told me my mother was with Anthony. I told the medium that Anthony was her father. My mother also told the medium that there are beautiful yellow flowers in heaven. The medium told me my mother was with another woman. I do not know who that would be. It could be her mother. Her real mother died when my mother was three years old. She died in childbirth in a New York City apartment house. I was able to have one of our relatives research my grandmother, and she told me that her name was Filomena Martorano Marra. She married Ciro Marra at St. Paul's Church in Manhattan when she was eighteen years old. She lived in a tenement building at 2 West Sixty-First Street and were still living in this building for the 1910 census in April. My grandmother died December 31, 1915, at a tenement at 2545 Eighth Avenue in Manhattan. She was twenty-three years, seven months, and one day old. She died from internal hemorrhage from the placenta, trauma, and shock. She was buried in Calvary Cemetery. My grandmother from my father's side was Angelina Giordano. She was born August 18, 1882, and died May 26, 1951.

Now let us continue with heaven. We all know there is a heaven. It is all around us and not just in one location. Some say it is in the fourth dimension. I am not too sure about this. I do know based on what I have seen here in this house that it is above us.

There is a theory in quantum physics that ten realms make up the spirit world. The universe is calculated to be made up of ten dimensions. Scientists say that these dimensions exist in the same space as the physical universe, much like boxes within a box. Near-death experiences will affirm that a multidimensional spirit world exists after death. This physical universe is one of these ten dimensions of reality, and humans are working their way up toward the highest heaven.

Our life on Earth is a preparation for our life in heaven. We come back to Earth for spiritual development and to bring the heaven we came from to Earth. It is also here on Earth that we and God can really know what level of spiritual development we desire and have earned. The level of our spiritual development determines which spiritual realm we will inhabit after death. We all have free will, and God does not force anyone to heaven. When we die, the physical body is gone, and now we step into the spiritual condition we have been building within us throughout our entire life. We all know that God is love, so the greater the spiritual love we build within us, the closer we are to God. As this holds true for the physical world, it holds true for the spirit world as well. It is a life of love that leads to heaven. We must learn to love one another.

Let's talk about spirit vibrations. Heaven is a matter of vibration, and the various realms after death are based on the various levels of spiritual energy that exist. As the quantum physicists say, the ten dimensions of reality exist within the same space as our universe and are based on the varying energy levels that exist. Just as we cannot see radio or television waves, we cannot see these multidimensional energy levels. Love is compared with heat, and these vibrations are finer than cold temperatures. The greater the love we have, the finer the vibration—and the closer we are to heaven and God. The heavier vibrations represent coldness, and the heavier the vibrations, the nearer we are to hell.

When we manifest unconditional love, our soul vibrations are so high that the only place we can fit into is heaven. Just like birds of a feather flock together, we gravitate after death into groups according to the rate of our soul's vibration.

Being on this Earth has given us some negative vibes, and we are at levels of discord after death. In heaven, God will remove these unwanted soul vibrations.

In the first stage of death, we are in a condition and acting according to the outward personality we had on Earth. We then slowly lose this outward personality consciousness and begin to become more of the person we actually are, according to our inner nature.

The further we get into the afterlife experience, the more we act on the basis of who we really are.

Now there is a final stage of the spirit world. This stage is called a stage of instruction. We must be instructed once again in the ways of the realm we have just entered. Time is not measured in this realm. Higher spirits will begin to educate us, and now bring us into heaven.

We now realize that we were merely visitors on Earth, and that heaven is our real home. We realize we have been in heaven before. Now knowledge beyond our deepest dreams exists all around us like the pervading music that can be heard. I heard the music of heaven when I saw my husband come down in shadow form. I heard the music for about one second, and then it stopped as he entered this world. Believe me, this music is beautiful—like chimes and harps playing at once. There are beautiful cities in heaven, libraries of wisdom, halls of spiritual learning, temples, and communities. Beautiful waterfalls, mountains, valleys, lakes, and other realms of recreation exist in heaven. There are also beautiful flowers in heaven. This knowledge is based on psychics and spirits telling mediums and psychics what is in heaven. My mother told a psychic I called that there are beautiful yellow flowers in heaven.

There is no time in the spirit world. We enjoy eternities in heaven. A soul can choose to remain in heaven for as long as desired and can choose to operate on that level of spiritual development forever. It is much harder to develop spiritually in heaven than in the physical realm. The soul's goal is to remain forever in heaven, and our goal is to bring heaven to Earth. We leave heaven to help our family and friends attain spiritual development. Our friends and family may exist on lower levels, and we leave paradise not just for the sake of our own spiritual development, but for those we love. We leave paradise for another incarnation at a lower spiritual level, but we will be brought home safely again. Ultimately, everyone will merge with God at the highest level as it was in the beginning.

This life on Earth is really a preparation for a fuller, freer, and richer external existence in heaven. It is much like a baby in the womb preparing to be born.

Regardless of our education, intelligence, wealth, or poverty, if we love unselfishly, our vibrations are so high that the only place we will fit into is heaven. We grow in heaven here on Earth based on our love for each other.

Let's talk about the journey in heaven.

1. A person leaves the body and enters into an earthbound realm where they can observe what is going on around the dead body.
2. The spirit may then be sucked into a tunnel toward the light, or find itself in a dark void temporarily until the tunnel appears.
3. Once the person is in the incredible light of God, they are overwhelmed by the love, beauty, happiness, and wonder of everything.

4. We now remember our forgotten knowledge, and supernatural powers are again realized, such as 360-degree vision, bilocation, instantaneous travel, mental telepathy, timelessness, heavenly music, creating realities with the mind, remembering past lives, omnipresence, time travel, seeing the future, meeting future children, and seeing orbs, angels, and guides.

5. The new arrival will be shown their life in review, for instructional purposes and for an evaluation to see if they have earned the right to enter a higher heavenly realm

6. There is a homecoming in heaven, and the person is reunited with family and friends.

7. Now the person will see the heavenly structures—cities and libraries of knowledge.

8. There are heavenly vistas such as exquisite valleys, gardens, lakes, rivers, mountains, waterfalls, and dwellings.

9. If the choice is to remain in heaven, then the new arrival is able to choose their habitation. It may be on a higher realm that they have earned, or they can operate at the same level or a lower level where loved ones may need help.

10. In heaven there is a World-School. In heaven, an Earth life seems to last for only a brief moment. After the moment in the World-School is over, the person goes through the process again to see if they have earned the right to a higher level of heavenly life.

In heaven you feel much more alive than you have ever felt before. Our lives on Earth are for just a short time, as though we were on a vacation. You visit and try to find your way around, and just when you think you've got it down, it's time to go home.

When going back to heaven, we may experience people who are yet to be born or are preparing to be born into the world.

In the highest realm of heaven, love reigns. When there is love, there is happiness.

All in all, it is our behaviors here on Earth that determine where we dwell in heaven. No one sends us anywhere after death. We are sorted by the vibration of the soul. Everyone goes where they will fit in. High vibrations indicate love and spiritual development. Low vibrations indicate debasement and evil.

In heaven, there is no time or space as we think it here. Heaven exists in a higher dimension of energy. The love of God is like the air we breathe. As air is the atmosphere on Earth, God's love is the atmosphere in the spirit world.

The spirit body can travel by thought. If one thinks of a person or place, one can immediately be transported there. Communication is also by thought, because in the spirit world, we are free from the restrictions of a physical body. I have a DVD of an orb entering this dimension. It was taken in the living room in January 2012. I can see the orb, and a few yards away from it is a light. This light vibrates with the orb. In the orb I can see my husband's face when he was young. It looks like trees or some type of land next to him. It is hard to really distinguish this, but I think it is the portal to heaven. You can buy this DVD and contact me on my website.

Married couples will be reunited after death. They may choose to stay together if they want to, provided they are on the same level of vibration. A physical body is of no use in the spiritual world. People in heaven get along very well with translucent spiritual bodies.

I will now talk about "vibrational rates." Just as our five physical senses are based on physical vibration, so our sixth sense is based on spiritual vibration. Our vibrational rate is like a frequency: the lower our vibrational rate becomes, the more physical our existence. As our vibrational rate or frequency increases, communication is possible with the spirit plane, and as our vibrational rate increases further, the higher plane is reached.

We are able to talk to God when our vibrational rate reaches a sufficient level. Spirit guides operate at a lower vibration than those on the higher plane but at a higher vibration than us while we are on the Earth plane.

To exist in physical form, we need to lower our vibrational rate, and to operate on the spiritual plane, we need to increase our vibrational rate.

Existence on the Earth plane slows our vibrational rate. The existence on this Earth plane prevents us from fully becoming part of the higher plane since the Earth plane slows our vibrational rate. Our conscious mind is physical. Our conscious mind belongs on this physical plane and ceases to exist with the body. We retain all that we have experienced as we cross into the spirit plane, which is governed by the subconscious mind. Again, when we take on a physical existence, our vibrating rate lowers. Our higher self, our superconsciousness, is that which is attached to the higher plane. Our superconsciousness is the part of us that is God. This is how God is within all, and how all are within God.

For spirits to enter this physical plane, they have to lower their vibrational rates. Spirits use shadows and reflections to camouflage themselves. The spirit needs to experience its ability to lower its vibrational rate and take on a physical appearance while it is between incarnations.

It is not uncommon for encounters with those on the spirit plane to have physical aspects, such as by touching a person (which has happened to me in my bedroom). I had a hand touch my face twice while I was in bed lying down. I had shingles on the right side of my face, and I think my husband tried to comfort me. These encounters are based on the same principle of the spirits lowering their vibrational rates.

Mental illness can be cured by increasing your vibrational rate. By increasing this vibrational rate, the permanent doorway to spirituality is opened. Our increased vibrational rate produces a change in the chemical balance within the brain. This chemical adjustment has been identified, and drugs have been produced to alter the changed chemical balance and reverse the effects, thus curing mental illness and returning those who suffer to normal.

If the chemical balance is reached by drugs, it is temporary, and lasts only as long as the drugs are maintained. Alcohol and drugs throw our vibrational rate out of balance. A higher vibrational rate deflects negativity. Even music can be used for healing as well as soothing us. We need to allow ourselves to feel the music, not just hear the music.

What is an aura? This is your soul. Our soul is not contained within the body, but our body is contained within our soul. Our aura reflects our true selves. It shows who we are. Our aura is our soul and a combination of light, color, and energy. This energy is in fact the very fabric of existence.

Each soul exists on its own vibrational frequency, which is unique to that soul. This is the soul's spiritual fingerprint.

We retain a connection with the places on the Earth plane where we have existed during our previous lifetimes. You have visited certain places in the world as though you have been there before or just love them. This is because in your previous lifetimes, this place was your home.

What about aliens—entities from another world? Some of the entities from other worlds who visit here can be transparent in form because of the different frequency of their vibrational rate. These entities are considered advanced souls.

Chapter 9

Purgatory

This place is a cleansing state for souls that are not ready for heaven. A modern name for purgatory is the void. There is a cleansing fire there. This notion of purgatory is associated particularly with the Catholic Church. In Catholic Church doctrine, all who die in God's grace and friendship but who are still imperfectly purified are assured of eternal salvation, but after death they must undergo a purification of the soul to achieve the holiness needed to enter the joy of heaven. This final purification of the soul is entirely different from the punishment of the damned.

The word *purgatory*, derived through Anglo-Norman and Old French from the Latin word *purgatorium,* has come to refer also to a wide range of historical and modern conceptions of postmortem suffering short of everlasting damnation. It is used in a nonspecific sense, to mean any place or condition of suffering or torment, especially one that is temporary. Encyclopaedia Britannica.

The afterlife played an important part in ancient Egyptian religion and culture. It was believed that when the body dies, parts of the soul known as *ka* (body double) and the *ba* (personality) go to the Kingdom of the Dead.

Arriving at one's reward in the afterlife was a demanding ordeal. You had to have a sin-free heart and the ability to recite the spells, passwords, and formula of the *Book of the Dead*. In the Hall of Two Truths, the deceased's heart was weighted against the Shu feather of truth and justice taken from the headdress of the goddess Ma'at. If the heart was lighter than the feather, they could pass on, but if it was heavier, they would be devoured by the demon Ammit.

In Egyptian religion, death was simply a temporary interruption, rather than a complete cessation of life.

There is also belief in reincarnation, which is widely accepted by the Ashkenazi Jews. They believe that some human souls could end up being reincarnated into nonhuman bodies. As I mentioned before, cats, dogs, and other animals have souls. By no means do all Jews today believe in reincarnation, but belief in reincarnation is not uncommon among many Jews, including Orthodox Jews. Most Orthodox prayer books have a prayer asking for forgiveness for one's sins that one may have committed in this gilgul or a previous one.

Reincarnation refers to an afterlife concept found among Hindus, Buddhists, Jains, Sikhs, Rosicrucians, Spiritists, and

Wiccans. In reincarnation, spiritual development continues after death and the deceased will begin another earthly life in the physical world. In reincarnation, the soul acquires a superior grade of consciousness and altruism by means of successive reincarnations.

In Christianity we believe in the Nicene Creed. "We look for the resurrection of the dead, and the life of the world to come."

Jesus compared the kingdom of heaven, over which He rules, to a net that was thrown into the sea and gathered fish of every kind. When it was full, men drew it ashore and sat down and sorted the good into vessels but threw away the bad. So it will be at the close of the age, also known as the Last Day. The angels will separate the evil from the righteous and throw them into the furnace of unquenchable fire. Then the righteous will shine like the sun in the kingdom of their Father.

In purgatory there are flames of purification. There is an after-death cleansing of the soul so that it can enter heaven. The Catholic conception of the afterlife teaches that after the body dies, the soul is judged, and the righteous and free of sin enter heaven. However, those who die in unrepented mortal sin go to hell. In the 1990s, the catechism of the Catholic Church defined hell not as punishment imposed on a sinner but rather as the sinner's self-exclusion from God. Unlike other Christian groups, the Catholic Church teaches that those who die in the state of grace but still carry venial sin go to a place called purgatory, where they undergo purification to enter heaven.

In the Hindu religion, the soul never dies. What dies is the body, which is made of five elements; earth, water, fire, air, and sky. The soul is believed to be indestructible. None of these five elements can ever harm or influence it. People with bad karma are punished after death in hell and dealt with accordingly.

The Hindus believe in karma. Karma is the accumulated sums of one's good and bad deeds here on Earth. The concept of karma is "As you sow, so you shall reap." If a person has lived a good life, they will be rewarded in the afterlife. Similarly the sum of bad deeds will be mirrored in their next life. Good karma brings good rewards, and bad karma leads to bad results.

Even Buddhists believe in good karma and bad karma. If a person committed harmful actions of body, speech, and mind based on greed, hatred, and delusion, rebirth will be in a lower realm—that is, in an animal, ghost, or hell realm. On the other hand, when a person has performed good deeds filled with generosity, loving kindness, compassion, and wisdom, rebirth will be in the heavenly realms.

So, all in all, each and every religion seems to believe that good deeds here on Earth will be rewarded and bad deeds will be punished.

When we die, the amount of justice or mercy with which we will be treated is up to us and depends on how merciful we ourselves have been. Jesus in his beatitudes said, "Blessed are the Merciful for they shall receive Mercy" (Matthew 5:7). All the beatitudes seem to apply to the next life. If we die repenting of our sins and have been very merciful and forgiving in our own lives, we will receive a lot of justice from God and be sent to purgatory for a certain length of time. When we recite the Lord's Prayer, we say the following:

Our Father,

Who art in Heaven,

Hallowed be Thy name,

Thy Kingdom come,

Thy Will be done on earth as it is in Heaven.

Give us this day our daily bread,

And forgive us our trespasses as we forgive those who

Trespass against us.

And lead us not into temptation,

but deliver us from evil. Amen.

Many people repent of their sins when they are dying because they are more afraid of going to hell than they are sorry for their sins. This is very wrong, because we should really be sorry for our sins only because they have hurt God, and we should want to suffer gladly for them. This repentance is imperfect, and God cannot give us total mercy and send us straight to heaven. This is where purgatory comes in. Purgatory is a reminder to us that we are *not* free to do any evil we like in this life and then just repent when we die, thinking we will go straight to heaven. No, this is not the case. God is not a God that wants us to suffer. He would rather pardon us than condemn us, but again this depends on us. When Jesus talked about "making up with your accusers before you get to court or else they will throw you into prison and you will not get out until you have paid the last penny" (see Matthew 5:26), this statement refers to purgatory.

The souls in purgatory cannot pray for themselves because they are under the justice of God, but we can pray for them and God will grant them mercy. I think these spirits and apparitions coming to my house are looking for help in getting out of purgatory. Some of them are very distraught and not at peace. This is why we must pray for the souls in purgatory when we go to Mass in the Catholic Church.

According to Catholic belief, immediately after death, a person undergoes judgment in which the soul's eternal destiny is specified. In purgatory, souls achieve the holiness necessary to enter the joy of heaven after purification.

Purgatory is a cleansing that involves painful temporal punishment, associated with the idea of fire and the eternal punishment of hell. There are images of purgatory in many books that depict souls being purified by flames. This state of purgatory does not mean a sad state for the soul but is really a positive state, because the soul is on its way to be with God. Prayers for the dead in purgatory decrease the length of time they spend there.

Where is purgatory anyway? Where is the physical plane of purgatory? Heaven and hell are regarded as places existing within the physical universe. Heaven is above us and hell is

below us. Hell could be in the Earth or beneath the Earth.
Purgatory has at times also been thought to be a physical
location. In 1999, Pope John II said that the term *purgatory*
does not indicate a place but "a condition of existence."

The purifying flames that are talked about in purgatory refer
to our soul suffering for having failed in the correct and
perfect way to God and His love. This becomes a flame, and
love itself cleanses the soul from the residue of sin. Of course,
these are the teachings of the Catholic Church and not other
religions. I talk here only about the Catholic Church and
purgatory since I am a Catholic.

According to Fr. F. X. Schouppe, S.J., in his book titled
Purgatory "when the souls in Purgatory visit the living,
they always present themselves in an attitude which excites
compassion; now with the features which they had during life
or at their death, with a sad countenance and imploring looks,
in garments of mourning, with an expression of extreme
suffering; then like a mist, a light, a shadow or some kind of
fantastic figure, accompanied by a sign or word by which they
may be recognized. At other times, they betray their presence
by moans, sobs, sighs, or a hurried respiration and plaintive
accents. They often appear enveloped in flames. When they
speak, it is to manifest their sufferings, to deplore their past
faults, to ask suffrages, or even to address reproaches to those
who ought to succor them. Another kind of revelation, adds
the same author, is made by invisible blows which the living
receive, by the violent shutting of doors, the rattling of chains,
and the sound of voices."

The above paragraph taken from Fr. F. X Schouppe's book is
absolutely correct. I have heard voices and rapid respiration of

the dead, and experienced many other strange occurrences in this house. Based on the above paragraph, I think these spirits are from purgatory and need help by means of praying for them.

Please pray for the souls in purgatory by reciting this prayer:

From the Holy Sacrifice of the Mass:

O most gentle Heart of Jesus, ever present in the Blessed Sacrament, even consumed with burning love for the poor captive souls in Purgatory, have mercy on the souls of Thy departed servants. Be not severe in Thy judgments, but let some drops of Thy Precious Blood fall upon the devouring flames. And do Thou, O Merciful Saviour, send thy holy angels to conduct them to a place of refreshment, light and peace. Amen.

O Mother most merciful, pray for the souls in Purgatory!

CHAPTER 10

HELL

Beware: Anyone who stops an individual from praying or going to church will spend his eternal life in hell!

Does hell exist? Absolutely. If you doubt it, please read the book *Beyond Death's Door* by Maurice Rawlings. Below is a paragraph from his book that depicts the terror of hell.

Dr. Rawlings is a specialist in internal medicine and cardiovascular disease and has resuscitated many individuals who were clinically dead. He is an atheist and once considered all religion "hocus-pocus" and death nothing more than a "painless extinction." He was resuscitating a man who was terrified and screaming because he was descending into the flames of hell. Here is what Dr. Rawlings wrote in his book:

Each time he regained heartbeat and respiration, the patient screamed, "I am in hell!" He was terrified and pleaded with me to help him. I was scared to death. Then I noticed a genuinely alarmed look on his face. He had a terrified look worse than the expression seen in death! This patient had a grotesque grimace expressing sheer horror! His pupils were dilated, and he was perspiring and trembling—he looked as if his hair was "on end."

Then still another strange thing happened. He said "Don't you understand? I am in hell . . . Don't let me go back to hell! . . .

. . . the man was serious, and it finally occurred to me that he was *indeed* in trouble. He was in a panic like I had never seen before. (Maurice Rawlings, *Beyond Death's Door*, Thomas Nelson Inc., 1979, p. 3).

If you read the Bible, you will see that it continually warns of a place called hell. There are more than 162 references in the New Testament alone that warn of hell. The Bible also tells of the location of hell. According to the Bible, hell is in the lower parts of the Earth. It is somewhere in the heart of the Earth itself and called "the pit" (Isaiah 14:9, 15; Ezekiel 32:18-21) and "the abyss" (Revelation 9:2).

In the book *Volcanoes: Earth's Awakening* an erupting volcano is described as "descent into HELL." Author is Katia Krafft (1980).

Thousands of years ago, the Bible described a place called hell in the heart of the Earth that matches exactly what science is now discovering.

Yes, there is definitely a place called hell!

"And the earth opened her mouth, and swallowed them up, and their houses, and all the men that appertained unto Korah, and all their goods. They, and all that appertained to them, went down alive into the pit, and the earth closed upon them" (Numbers 16:32-33).

There was a famous fourteenth-century astronomer and physician whose name was Caspar Peucer. He researched and documented volcano eruptions around the world. Peucer claimed (as others have) that "fearful howlings, weeping and gnashing of teeth could be heard" for many miles as the volcanoes erupted:

"Out of the bottomless abyss of Hekiafell, or rather out of Hell itself, rise melancholy cries and loud wailings, so that these can be heard for many miles around . . . there may be heard in the mountain fearful howlings, weeping and gnashing of teeth." (Haraldur Sigurdsson, *Melting the Earth, The History of Ideas on Volcanic Eruptions, 1999,* p. 73)

People have claimed to hear "cries and screaming" coming from volcanoes. They simply explain them as the "sounds of hell."

"The fearsome noises that issued from some of their volcanoes were certainly thought to be the screams of tormented souls in the fires of hell below" (Sigurdsson, p. 73).

According to Mark 9:46, Jesus Christ describes hell as a place "where their worms dieth not, and the fire is not quenched."

Scientists have recently discovered cracks on the ocean floor where fire was leaking out. Eight-foot-long worms were found in no other place in the world. The book *The Deep Sea,* by Joseph Wallace, says, "Perhaps the strangest of ocean creatures recently discovered are Rifitia, the giant tube WORMS. Measuring up to 8 feet in lengththe worms are Only FOUND NEAR THE DEEP SEA VENTS" (P. 39).

These quotes are from some good books, and of course, the Bible talks about the reality of hell. We all pretend to ignore these revelations, but hell does exist! We all know it.

Revelation 14:10 says, "and he shall be tormented with fire and brimstone." Job 18:21 describes hell as the "place of him that knoweth not God" and says in verse 15 that "brimstone shall be scattered upon his habitation." Brimstone is sulfur. Sulfur, or brimstone, is found inside the Earth.

Nature magazine recently discovered (July 2002) what the Bible knew more than 3,000 years ago: inside this Earth is "fire and brimstone."

It is humanly impossible to comprehend the Bible description of hell. Read your Bible! Nothing on Earth can compare with it. No nightmare could produce a terror like hell. No horror movie can describe its fright.

The Bible warns in Psalm 9:17 that you will not only be in hell but will be turned into hell. You will literally be hell!

All who enter hell, abandon all hope!

In Finland, researchers recorded the screams of the damned. In a Finnish newspaper called *Ammenusastia,* a scientist whose name was Dr. Azzacove was quoted as saying, "Needless to say we were shocked to make such a discovery. But we know what we saw and we know what we heard. And we were absolutely convinced that we drilled through the gates of hell!" His account continues as follows:

> The drill suddenly began to rotate wildly, indicating that we had reached a large empty pocket or cavern. Temperature sensors showed a dramatic increase in heat to 2,000 degrees Fahrenheit.

> We lowered the microphone, designed to detect the sounds of plate movements down the shaft. But instead of plate movements we heard a human voice screaming in pain! At first we thought the sound was coming from our own equipment.

> But when we made adjustments our worst suspicions were confirmed. The screams weren't those of a single human, they were the screams of millions of humans!

Remember, God is a God of love but also a holy God. A holy God will demand payment for sin. Because God is holy, sin *must* be condemned. Joshua 24:19 says, "He is a Holy God . . . he will not forgive your transgressions nor your sins."

God does not send someone to hell. It is the person who chooses hell when they reject Jesus Christ. When you refuse God's love gift of eternal life in Jesus Christ, you choose hell!

All of you who are reading my book, please bow your head this minute and ask the Lord Jesus Christ to save you. Do not put this off another second! Three people die every second, 180 every minute. Since you started reading my book, 2,000 more people have gone into eternity. It could have been an auto accident, a heart attack, a stroke, or something else. One thing is certain: you will die. It could be today, tomorrow, in a week, a month, a year, five years, ten years, or twenty years. Please be prepared.

I think I was chosen to write this book along with my other book, *You Can't Control the Soul,* to let people know that yes, there is an afterlife. The soul never dies! We go to either heaven, purgatory, or hell. Please, everyone reading this book, do everything you can to be saved and not go to hell. This is my reason for writing this book. If I can help save one soul, I will feel that I have been put on this Earth for a purpose. I feel that this is why I was saved from drowning when I was ten years old. A spiritual hand pulled me up from the bottom of the pool and saved me. I am here for a purpose, as you all are. Jesus Christ, our savior, wants us all to enjoy the beauty of heaven for all eternity. I hope you all go to heaven!

God bless you all!